THE
SATANIC WARLOCK

Magister Dr. Robert Johnson

HAIL THE SATANIC WARLOCK!

Are they modern-day sorcerers, seducers, or the new Black Guard of Satanism? Only the Devil knows! A Warlock's wicked ways have always held the secret blueprints to becoming his own god. Many extraordinary men have joined Anton LaVey's Church of Satan in the past 50 years, establishing Satanism as the   religion that continues to shock and intrigue the world. This "man's manual" unleashes their undefiled Satanic wisdom on the world.

Magister Dr. Robert Johnson's long-awaited counterpart to LaVey's *The Satanic Witch* is being heralded as the definitive manual for the 21st Century Satanic man.

Here's a magical book to titillate as well as inform, unlock the secrets of sex and seduction, and define magic in true Satanic fashion.

LEARN THE HIDDEN SECRETS OF SATANIC SEDUCTION!

Magister Johnson holds a doctorate in human sexuality, sharing his decades of experience as a leading member of the Church of Satan, publisher of *Old Nick* magazine, executive at Playboy Enterprises, and real-world connoisseur of the human sexual condition. This book shares his priceless insights into every aspect of what makes a Warlock tick.

First-hand accounts from practicing Satanic Warlocks and Witches reveal the truth about these citizens of the Infernal Empire – how they think, what they do, and what secrets they employ to seduce any lover they choose!

People are talking...

How does a genuine practitioner of Satanic magic cast a persuasive spell to get a date, attract a playmate, or win a woman's heart? Let the King of the Naked Witches explain it all to you! Magister Bob Johnson, Doctor of Satanic Sex, will clue you in on the Devil's secret pickup techniques, while helping you use your existing strengths to identify areas of improvement. Become the Warlock you have always wanted to be; let the Master help you gain the confidence to go forth, conquer, and create your own world in the Here and Now.

– Peggy Nadramia, High Priestess of the Church of Satan

Doktor said, "There is a beast in man that should be exercised, not exorcised." Though this is an inspiring quote, no book existed to spell out this undefiled wisdom – until now.

This indispensible guide musters and serves up the tools and secrets of the Satanic Warlock. Men must stand up and retake what we have collectively given away: our masculinity. This unapologetic treatise is essential for any Satanic Warlock. Stoke your Black Flame.

– Reverend Campbell, Church of Satan

This is the book Anton LaVey resisted writing... he didn't want to give all his secrets away. Bob Johnson absorbed many of those secrets in hours of conversation with the perverse High Priest. He generously adds some secrets of his own, informed by his years in the porn and pulchritude game. This book reveals the sexual dance at its most satisfying – frank, musky, naughty, and erotically compelling. Settle back, pour yourself a scotch, and get schooled by your sensual sensei.

And ladies, prepare to be wickedly enchanted by the true Satanic Warlock who will apply these principles with finesse. He will haunt your dreams.

– Blanche Barton, Magistra Templi Rex of the Church of Satan

APERIENT PRESS

THE
SATANIC WARLOCK

Magister Dr. Robert Johnson

Edited by Ruth Waytz

THE SATANIC WARLOCK

TheSatanicWarlock.com

information@TheSatanicWarlock.com

Hardcover Limited Edition ISBN: 978-0-9712374-0-7
Paperback Edition ISBN: 978-0-9712374-4-5
e-book ISBN: 978-0-9712374-5-2

APERIENT PRESS
2118 Wilshire Blvd. #997
Santa Monica CA 90403-5784

Design by Theo Kouvatsos

Illustrations by D.S. Wallace aka Dorian Grey

Photos by Lorie Loupe

The official trademarked Baphomet image is used throughout
with permission from the Church of Satan.

Publisher's gratitude to The Maestro and the Muse

DEDICATION

For my father, who showed me the way,
and who, thankfully, I've become.

 CONTENTS

Acknowledgments

Introduction

Prologue

Preface

CHAPTER ONE • 1
What is a 21st Century Warlock?

CHAPTER TWO • 19
Warlock Archetypes

CHAPTER THREE • 44
Creating the Warlock Self

CHAPTER FOUR • 65
The Satanic Gentleman – "A Man of Wealth and Taste"

CHAPTER FIVE • 79
The Satanic Laws of Power – How to be a God!

CHAPTER SIX • 93
The Secret Art of Satanic Seduction

CHAPTER SEVEN • 145
Sex Magic (The Warlock as Sex Magician)

CHAPTER EIGHT • 159
The Gay Satanic Warlock

CHAPTER NINE • 169
The High Priestess Speaks!

AUTHOR'S AFTERWORD

Bibliography

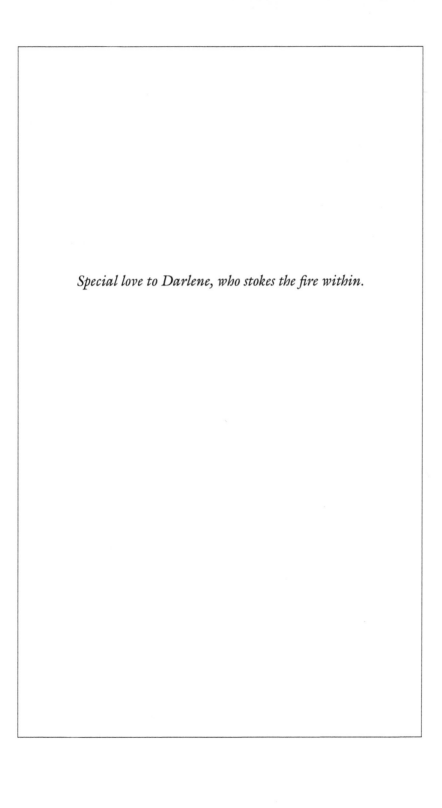

Special love to Darlene, who stokes the fire within.

ACKNOWLEDGMENTS

First and foremost I would like to thank my dear friends and mentors, the Maestro, Church of Satan High Priest Magus Peter H. Gilmore, and the brilliant and lovely High Priestess, Magistra Peggy Nadramia, for their unrelenting support, endorsement, and guidance. Without their razor-sharp vision and sovereign sanction, this book would never join Church of Satan canon.

I must also thank Magistra Templi Rex Blanche Barton for her encouragement, pedigree Satanic wisdom, and unique insights into what truly makes a Warlock.

My deep gratitude to my publishing partner and sister in sin, Magistra Ruth Waytz of Aperient Press, who edited the crap out of my diabolical ramblings.

Much loving thanks to my local Satanic family, including Priestess Marilyn Mansfield, Witch Karen Millman, Magister Joe Netherworld, Priest Zoth Ommog, and Magister Neil Smith.

My heartfelt appreciation to all of the Church of Satan Magisters, Magistras, Witches, Priests, Priestesses and members who contributed in words and deeds, including Warlock Aden Ardennes, Satanist Scarlett Black, Priest Adam Campbell, Priest Adam Cardone, Priest Lee Crowell, Priest Darren Deicide, Reverend Entity and Priestess FiFi, Priest Andrew James Ferris, Magister Lex Frost, Warlock Gyps Fulvus, Priest Nathan Gray, Warlock Dorian Grey, Magister David Harris, Witch Heather Height, Warlock David Ingram, Magister Robert Lang and Magistra Diana DeMagis, Priest Michaelanthony Mandrake, Magister Robert Merciless, the Count and Countess MoriVond, Magister Nemo, Priest John Shaw, Witch Hydra M. Star, Warlock G. Edwin Taylor, and the many stalwart citizens of the Infernal Empire who allowed me to bend their ears.

And certainly, the Black Pope himself, Magus Anton Szandor LaVey, whose dark inspiration lives on and guides us all.

INTRODUCTION

Conjuring Concupiscence – Empowering The Satanic Warlock

Anton Szandor LaVey's *The Compleat Witch* came forth into a world in the throes of social upheaval, at a time wherein gender roles were being questioned and reshaped as a means for greater individual autonomy – ostensibly. However, as with any nascent revolution, collective goals often force lock-step behavior which might present new avenues, but often at the expense of older roads well travelled but not willfully forsaken. Change does not favor all perspectives, and legions of babies are typically tossed out with oceans of bathwater that may still serve those thriving under the old regimes. Enter Dr. LaVey whose iconoclastic Church of Satan had been smashing spiritual paradigms by providing a carnal religion whose essential atheism embraced the human need for metaphor via dramatic, Infernal symbolism and cathartic ritual. It offered a means for living a life unhampered by frustrations as one celebrated one's individual proclivities, explored within reason and moderation amongst consenting open-minded adults.

Dr. LaVey was an outsider who pursued a number of off beat ways to generate income, from freelance police photography to psychic investigation, before he founded a religion and became an author. He debunked the supernatural, in the process discovering that people often preferred the irrationality of believing in spiritual causes rather than the mundane sources of their anxiety. He played music in nightclubs, carnivals and tent revivals absorbing nuances of human behavior fueled by desire and the resultant guilt coming from its satiation. He also taught "Witches Workshops" wherein what he defined as "Lesser Magic" – the wile, guile and charm used to attain one's desired ends – could be uniquely wielded by women. These tried and true methods were practical enchantments, as the men who fell for them were mostly blind to being so readily manipulated. Thus was Satanism devised as an antidote for theism-fostered repression – a means to fulfill the full range of human needs.

As the "sexual revolution" was being waged, LaVey noted that many proponents of feminism sought equity with males, who were condemned as being adversaries, yet the methodology often demanded that women become like their opposition. Many women found this liberating, while others felt it robbed them of the power inherent in their sex, which had been used for millennia with great success. The progressives would demean their sisters, calling them servile and outmoded for holding onto their old witcheries, but that did not stop those who had obtained their ends through the uniquely feminine artifices which offer dominion over most receptive males.

Dr. LaVey taught that all women could combine elements of sex, sentiment and wonder, to cultivate a personal look that could move men to do their bidding, from the bedroom to the boardroom. By celebrating the puissance of distaff pulchritude, he raised consciousness and pride for a third-side cadre of Amazons on the battlefields of this revolutionary landscape: The Satanic Witches. They sallied forth under the banner of Satanism, and reaped the benefits of true magic, much more ancient than any secrets claimed to be inherent in neo-paganism's various sects of witchcraft. And, unlike those various heathen reboots, in Satanism the term "Warlock" was readily employed for males with the testicular fortitude and magical sensibility to practice carnal sorcery and move the world according to their wills. LaVey had provided his most personal book as a guide to "Lesser Magic" for women who were drowning in societal tides hell-bent on quashing centuries of feminine methodologies. He did not see the need to do the same for men, but believed his Warlocks could benefit from the wisdom he imparted to Witches, to either resist or embrace their womanly cunning.

Now, more than four decades later, we have witnessed the metamorphosis of masculinity, again offering additional avenues but curtailing some classic modes of manliness. While in the time of *The Compleat Witch*, the word gender was used as a "polite" synonym for one's biological sex, now both words have been sundered. A veritable panoply of gender identifications is now emerging, allowing for individual tailoring. Archetypes are in protean flux and younger people might be confused as to their own identity as they enter the fray of sexual exploration—from dating and lovemaking to relationship building and family. Models are diverse, but also often dilute. With social media the commonly embraced tool for interaction, we see apps in use upon which cutthroat decisions are made in an instant as to who might be considered a beddable candidate. How to make a vital impression that opens gates to both erotic and emotional possibilities is often unclear.

Enter Dr. Robert Johnson, sexologist and exponent of piquing male lust in the many venues via which pornography has thrived, and Magister in the Church of Satan. His lifetime is one spent with a finger on the throbbing pulse of human lust in all its forms, using his wisdom and wizardry to evoke stimulation for thousands. As a compadre to Magus Anton Szandor LaVey and long time colleague of my own, his mastery of the principles of Satanic Magic, both Greater and Lesser, is assured. He has walked amongst Warlocks and tapped them for their personal techniques while refining his own diabolical expertise over a media-spanning career as a purveyor of lasciviousness. From this diverse background emerges his unique vision concerning contemporary masculinity and how it may be honed to serve Warlocks of the early 21st Century.

Here he offers distilled wisdom, ammunition for men to go forth and conquer the partners of their sensual dreams. It is intended for those who embrace the moniker of Warlock–a powerful, shadowy figure who has obtained forbidden secrets and exploits them for his own lusty conquests. Dr. Johnson reveals potent methods of self-definition for the dauntless male to stand forth from the herd and win his chosen quarry. He offers arcane erudition that bold men will take up to enhance their skills at seduction. And he recounts his own escapades, both triumphs and retreats, revealing his unique journey through the realms of sex, Satanism, and devilish debauchery. Enter freely, of your own will, and enjoy the license to Epicurean licentiousness that is at your fingertips.

– Magus Peter H. Gilmore

PROLOGUE

I WARLOCK or My Wicked, Wicked Ways

As a Warlock and a gentleman, I always love meeting new people, especially because I never tire of hearing "Please allow me to introduce myself" roll off my tongue. This otherwise innocuous phrase carries a delightfully Satanic overtone, thanks to the Rolling Stones' "Sympathy For the Devil." It has served me well over the years, as friends and family alike recognize it as my calling card.

So who am I? What gives me such audacity? You're absolutely right to demand my credentials. As the mason cementing the next layer of modern Satanic bedrock, I proudly offer my personal and professional CV – my "chops" if you will.

I'm recognized inside and outside the Church of Satan as a man who walks the walk. I don't mind if you don't know me, but please don't think the accomplishments, education, professional prowess, numerous love affairs, or rank of Church of Satan Magister herein are crowing, bragging or self-serving bravado. It's all true.

You may be dubious or even jealous. That's ok. But would you put much stock in this kind of vital, essential advice if it came from a pasty bookworm academic, new age pickup artist (PUA), or unlaid wannabe when you can get confidence and power straight from the Devil's mouth?

You may not like this book. That's ok too. *The Satanic Warlock* is my "is-to-be," transforming from idea to reality on the 50th anniversary of the Church of Satan.

A little history:

Of course, like many Witches and Warlocks, reading *The Satanic Bible* in my uber-horny teens was my first moment of pure crystallization to Satanism, probably because *here was a church that had naked girls as altars!*

And while the promise of sex got my attention, it is the philosophy which backed up those promises with real ideas that still resonates with me to this day. The titillation started by this notorious Church grew and propagated deep in the recesses of my being. A religion that celebrated sex and dismissed bullshit pie-in-the sky deities was intoxicating in itself, and the idea of being part of such a movement informed everything I did, from adolescence on.

These principles laid the groundwork for me as a man, and more importantly as a Satanic man. My Warlock identity was not the result of a conferred station or official title (which of course came later), but instead what it actually meant to be a member of the Church; to be recognized as one who defies herd mentality and makes his way in the world, thinking, acting, and flourishing as a true Warlock. The lycanthropic metamorphosis permeated my work, play, and relationships.

I met Anton LaVey and Blanche Barton at the San Francisco Black House in the early 1990s and was forever changed. Over the years, I read more of the official Satanic canon, including *The Compleat Witch*, *The Satanic Rituals*, *Secret Life of a Satanist*, and later my dear friend and mentor Magus and High Priest Peter H. Gilmore's *The Satanic Scriptures*, among other Satanic works. The transformation from ordinary man to Warlock progressed, forged in my devilish DNA. My circle of friends expanded to include more Church members, sharing experiences through often very intimate exchanges, broadening and solidifying my Satanic persona. This glue fused my Satanic self to my Warlock foundation, bringing me priceless and unique insights into the true meaning of "Satanic Warlock."

I won't even try to count the wonderful hours spent with High Priest Gilmore and his lovely and brilliant wife, High Priestess Peggy Nadramia, metaphorically drinking in their undefiled wisdom, often while *literally* drinking in some top shelf booze. My Warlock Self continues to mature.

Outside the Church, I've been a professional editor, writer, and publisher of men's magazines including *High Society, Cheri, Playgirl* (for gay men), and *Old Nick* (of course). I've been applying Satanic principles to real-world carnal situations for more than 30 years and making a damn good living at it.

I've also been an Executive Producer for Playboy Enterprises and an integral part of porn film powerhouse Vivid Entertainment's online presence.

All of these experiences – the majority of which are purely sex-centric – have given me a unique perspective on the human condition, especially regarding the mating game. Time and again I have witnessed the undeniable sexual driving force as it applies to all manners of love and romance, and seen how the Satanic Warlock ultimately operates.

This may seem like a narrow view of the overall human condition, especially when it comes to sexuality, seduction, and the power of attraction, but I can assure you my research represents a microcosm of what goes on in the real world. The red card I carry as a Satanist only reinforces the power of the Satanic perspective!

The common man often stumbles and appears weak, falling victim to the "power of the pussy/pecker" and sacrificing his own common sense and self interest to someone else's sexual power. In contrast, the trained and cognizant Warlock is nobody's victim: He has the tools to win his desired mate, or at least enjoy all the fruits of a completely satisfying pairing while the fun lasts.

Earning my bread and butter in the world of seduction allowed me to enjoy (and believe me, I *enjoyed*) participating in every possible scenario: simple romances with friends, office affairs, dating professional models, burlesque dancers, porn stars, sex workers, and even a few wives (often requiring sitcom-like escape scenarios from closets, hiding in cars, or exiting through second-story windows). The ultimate seductresses, of course, are always the Satanic Witches.

As a Magister in the Church of Satan, I've served as confidant to a host of people whose relationships range from delightful to disastrous.

I have also been a consulting copywriter for the Stylelife organization, the company spawned by Neil Strauss's *The Game – Penetrating the Secret Society of Pickup Artists* and *Rules of the Game*. These are commonly accepted as the preeminent books on the current PUA techniques. I've spent time in the heads of young men whose daily "work" involved finding and bedding women (and men). I lived in Los Angeles and wrote powerful "pickup advice" advertising campaigns. Strauss chronicled the masters of the game, including PUA legends "Mystery" and Ross Jeffries. In fact, Jeffries still includes "Magick" in some of his seminars – a tactic true Satanists know well and use every day. Except we spell it right and call it *Lesser Magic*.

My writing credits include articles on sex and Satanism for *Penthouse* and *High Society* magazines, among many others. I have written two books on the occult use of magic including *Corporate Magick, Mystical Tools for Business Success* (Kensington Publishing). This Greater Magic manual is a fiendishly clever nod to Satanic principles (customized for the herd), and was recently listed by *Esquire* Magazine as one of the books that should under no circumstances be displayed in one's office library – along with *The Prince* by Machiavelli and *The Secret* by Rhonda Byrne. A dubious honor for sure, but not bad literary company!

I also published *Occult Investigator: Real Cases From the Files of X-Investigations*, an investigation of paranormal claims in conjunction with a well-known New York City private investigations company. My acumen in this field comes, in great part, from having the distinct honor and joy of working with preeminent ghost hunter extraordinaire, the late Dr. Hans Holzer.

These experiences, plus working as a "real" journalist for newspapers and trade magazines – not just girlie and "sophisticate" stuff – honed my research skills to a fine, laser-focused point.

I'm proud to say my decades of reading, writing, and disseminating information about human carnal proclivities did not go unnoticed. In 2014, I was awarded a Doctorate in Human Sexuality from the Institute of Advanced Study of Human Sexuality (IASHS) in San Francisco. I am currently studying to be a Certified Sex Coach with Sex Coach University.

I've nearly drowned in epicurean and hedonistic delights, from the Hollywood Hills to the mountains of Transylvania to Italy's Amalfi Coast. And unlike celebrities blessed with striking good looks, riches, or great talent, I am a rather average fellow in looks and intelligence. Of course, I am armed with something much more powerful, magical, and awe-inspiring: I'm a natural born Satanist!

I've used this innate power and understanding of what a true Warlock is to navigate corporate boardrooms and beautiful women's bedrooms with a style and confidence that always eludes the herd. I've enjoyed soirees and after-parties at the Playboy Mansion and lost track of how many nubile models and would-be actresses graced those evenings. I've indulged at the Bunny Ranch, one of the legal brothels in Nevada, where every kink, fetish, and erotic experience is for sale. All these adventures have given me a pure understanding of true carnality and indulgence – the very cornerstones of Satanism.

I've probably gone into more detail here than necessary, but accomplished Warlocks know they need to anticipate and silence their critics. I'm happy to serve a hot bowl of *shut the fuck up* to anyone who reads this book looking to find fault or whine that I didn't cover their particular kink. Think I don't know what I'm talking about? My data comes from decades of study and personal Satanic experience.

My Satanic friends often call me "The Chairman" because of my love for the late Frank Sinatra and my affinity for the 1960s Rat Pack era. That term is universal, but Sinatra actually referred to his crew as "the Clan", "The Summit", and of course "Brother Rats". I can't sing for my supper, but we do have a lot in common: wearing tuxedos, drinking Jack Daniels until we're petrified, and hanging out in the company of saucy, good-looking broads for instance. Back in the 1990s, a few of my own "Rat Packers" and I were in a New York bar, dressed to the nines and making a night of it. We were approached by a group of older lovelies (borderline MILFs, not grannies on walkers) who said we reminded them of that bygone era. That cemented it. From then on I knew my calling, crystallizing the attitude I used even as I wrote this book. Of course I may have had a little help from Old Blue Eyes himself – much of the writing was done while listening to Sinatra's signature song ... "My Way."

Understanding what physically and psychologically goes on in all interpersonal relationships (including the mating game) gives me unique insight into how the Warlock navigates what is undeniably our most complex set of circumstances. Warlocks are human, but remain mindful of Anton LaVey's instruction to appreciate and learn from our four-legged friends. And despite the idiotic but persistent politically correct fallacy that men and women are completely equal, men are different – really different – than women and are unapologetically not equal with regard to some of our less-than-flattering traits.

Men are dogs. Warlocks are werewolves. Nearly all our drives, ambitions, and accomplishments are ego-based attempts to appear virile and powerful. Guess why?

Men, despite being (on average) physically stronger, are more aggressive, narcissistic, and self-indulgent and have shorter life spans. And dear brothers, anthropologically speaking, we really do have just one job: to fuck as much as possible and propagate the species. Call it caveman thinking or straight up sexism, but no rational person can argue convincingly against it.

And by understanding what a Warlock truly is and applying the magical principles and tools we all possess, I'll say I have accomplished things so truly amazing I have even surprised and shocked myself! Places I never thought I'd see, women I never thought would give me the time of day, and material pleasures that seemed unobtainable, all came to me as naturally as breathing. As above, so below. That my friend is real magic!

So I submit to you, my comrades, brothers, and fellow followers of all things diabolical, this *grimoire*, in hope that you take this Devilish wisdom to heart and practice, practice, practice the secrets of the true Warlock. Join me in the Hellfire Brotherhood, forged by the great Satanic minds of the last 50 years. As Magus Gilmore said, "Satan is the symbol that best suits the nature of who we are, carnal by birth."

So come all ye Priests of Mendes, brave followers of the Left Hand Path, magicians, scoundrels, rogues, poets, free thinkers, and men of means both material and magical! Explode into the new century, heads held high as *Satanic Warlocks* – true gods among men!

PREFACE

"HAIL THE SATANIC WARLOCK"

Satanic Warlocks are the last bastion of real masculinity and power. Warlocks are confident in what they do and reject political correctness for the sake of societal acceptance. We believe it's still a man's world (in whatever context) and are fully aware that savvy women can easily manipulate us – which is just how we like it!

Before Anton Szandor LaVey released his groundbreaking and diabolical handbook for the Satanic woman (*The Compleat Witch*) popular culture knew (or should we say discussed) little to nothing about women using their natural wiles and charms to get what they wanted. Drawing from lifelong observations of the world (and underworld) around him, LaVey was the first to codify such an incendiary guidebook, giving women both the license and the means to fulfill their wildest desires. It was the 1960s, and *The Compleat Witch* was a lynchpin in the Satanic cultural revolution. The Establishment was put on trial, and savvy Satanists raised a middle finger with gusto. A new trail was blazed – with hellfire – and a very sexy handbook was forged by a real man's man, to the delight of real women everywhere.

As Magistra Blanche Barton wrote in *The Secret Life of a Satanist*, LaVey introduced an antidote to the feminist fervor of the times – what he called "the most aesthetically barren period in history."

This was no *Good Housekeeping* "10 Tips to a Happy Hubby" claptrap, scribbled by some Vassar-schooled editorial assistant whose real-life experience in getting a man (or anything else) likely began and ended with her letting her English Lit professor finger her in some seedy teachers' lounge to get her from a C- to a B+.

No, this was pure Satanic know-how, straight from LaVey's firsthand observations at carnivals and burlesque venues; the garden of carnal delights that codified modern Satanism. A clarion call, awakening the Witches of the world to embrace the awesome powers they'd heard whispers about but never believed they possessed.

Finally, women had a practical guide for seduction in both their personal lives and their careers. The many who eschewed bra burning (but liked sexual freedom) and who didn't "make it" with just any sandal-wearing hippie (but enjoyed the pleasures of as many lovers as they chose) now had the ways and means to really blossom. LaVey's magic was at their fingertips, and their power became limitless.

LaVey aptly defined the woman who employed these magical tactics and thus created the Satanic Witch, showing girls that they were both savvy women and seductresses. Combining the two created a succubus of unbridled passion, prepared to get whatever she desired. For the first time in history, the Satanic siren was liberated, replacing the tired stereotype of ugly and malicious hag. A few "sexy witches" graced October calendar pages, films and TV shows, ("Bewitched," "Bell Book & Candle"), but the term "witch" still carried an overwhelmingly negative (cold as a witch's tit) connotation.

But that all changed with *The Compleat Witch* – a simple yet compelling roadmap of the principles of attracting, seducing, and – dare we say – manipulating men (or partners) of their choice in the pursuit of carnal and other desires.

This liberating and revolutionary Satanic tract shocked even the feminist-leaning free thinkers of the time, resonating with an entire underserved sector of the world's female population: those who identified with the dark aesthetic and reveled in the pleasures of the flesh. These girls finally had license to practice what they instinctively knew but often repressed, either out of ignorance or an overwhelming sense of taboo dictated by society. It was about time!

LaVey's much-needed gift to women set free a firestorm of female power that's been percolating for decades and given many lucky men a taste of what a real woman can do – both in and out of bed!

And needless to say, any man who has sampled the pleasures of a Satanic Witch (officially or de facto) can surely attest to the incredible delights these women offer. LaVey's book not only provided a valuable tool for these lovely enchantresses, but its "long tail" gave men a gift of unparalleled pleasure. Those of us who had the honor and pleasure of knowing LaVey can easily believe with a wink and a nod that the Black Pope's underlying intention was always twofold: give the girls tips on living life to the fullest … and let the boys enjoy the results! As a self-proclaimed misogynist who admired the power of sexy women, LaVey reminded the world that men and women are *very different* and that the inversion/perversion of the sexual roles to suit a feminist active/passive dynamic was a sham. Men were thrust into a stupor and women were forced to be more aggressive, even if it wasn't their natural proclivity.

The good news is that, intentional or not, the Satanic man has had it quite a bit easier when lucky enough to partner with a Satanically schooled Witch. The girls may choose to hide their magic and their "commands to look" (and touch!), but more savvy beaus will see the wiles at work and probably not care, as long as they get the result they want. What could be better?

THE TIME OF THE WARLOCK

Which brings us to the rub, bub… that you've been sitting on your asses and enjoying these Satanic Witches far too long. Some of you are taking your fill of the fruits of the Witch – often blindly – while others are out in the cold, scratching their heads and wondering, "Where's *my* witch? How come *I'm* not gettin' any?" Well fella, real world rules apply to Satanists too.

If we want to *get*, we first have to *do*. We must perform our magic and initiate our "is-to-be" by using our strengths and smarts if we want to partake of the fruits we lust after. We must identify the objects of our desire, recognize what tools are at our disposal, build our charisma, and above all *practice!* Of course, all Warlocks will at some time have what they want simply drop in their laps with no hard work, but don't make that your only strategy. In the real (and only) world, that rarely happens.

Although "Warlock" is a specific title within the Church of Satan, the term will be used here to mean the male counterpart to the Witch. This book will identify and define what a true Warlock is, how he should walk in the world, and also serve as a primer on seduction – one of his most prized skills.

Even now, a multitude of men (Satanists included) still have woman trouble. They find themselves mired in a woman's web, either as slaves to their schwantzes, or just not able to get in the game. They know a wonderful world of debauchery is happening all around them; they just can't close a deal. The good news is that these abilities are inherent – they simply need to be unlocked.

The past 50 years have fully established Satanism as the sanest and most and liberating religion on earth, and the Church of Satan has attracted myriad followers who embrace the carnal in all its many delightful forms. Satanic Witches have wasted no time honing their skills. Smart Satanic men have made it their business to read *The Compleat Witch* (aka *The Satanic Witch*), to peek under their skirts and see what the girls have been up to. Some have mastered the ability to navigate the tricky waters of seduction and relationships in true Warlock fashion, using these books and their own instincts. You know who you are, and where you fit – or maybe you don't? But fear not. A refresher course is at hand. It's time to "man up" and grasp the true power of the Satanic Warlock in all his forms.

This book finally codifies the conventional wisdom of the last five decades. Not that anyone was deliberately keeping secrets; we all just assumed the Satanic man – the Warlock – already had a strong identity and diabolical role models, and, frankly, that he was just too damned masculine to need a guidebook to tell him how to move through his world. The idea of a "man's manual" – so to speak, struck many as unnecessary. Men don't ask for directions, men don't need doctors, men are strong and independent. Men just figure it out. This has especially been true for freethinking, rebellious Satanic men who march to their own drummers. Good for them … to a point.

Unlike the budding pre-1960s Satanic Witch, unaware of her charms and wiles and eager to be shown her Satanic powers, many Warlocks think they already know everything. They think they know how to act, how to seduce, and how to use Satanic principles along with Lesser and Greater Magic, simply because they embrace the Satanic philosophy. The wolf, metaphoric kin to many Satanic men, prevails in the wild without guidance, says the Warlock. But not so fast: even the fearsome predator was once a cub – a fact that must never be overlooked.

As much of a "manly man" as a Warlock knows he is (and many do fit at 12 o'clock on LaVey's *Satanic Witch* Personality Synthesizer), it's a sure bet that only a small portion are always the "macho guy" they display to the world. Whether or not they want to admit it, Warlocks are also vulnerable, never more so than in the arenas of love, seduction, and relationships. A 2014 *Psychology Today* post revealed that, on average, men don't handle breakups nearly as well as women. Men depend more on their partners for emotional stability and support, so when it's over they crawl back to their caves to lick their wounds. Findings showed heterosexual men don't sleep as well away from their partners and they tend to fall into bad habits after a breakup. When asked whom they would turn to first if they felt depressed, 71 percent of men said their spouse or significant other, whereas only 39 percent of women made the same choice.

It's a man thing for sure: we don't have women's strong verbal communication network and we don't often share our emotions. In fact, some research suggests that men are neurochemically predisposed to having a tough time without a love interest, compromised by reduced levels of oxytocin (the hormone that fuels love and lust).

Of course the Warlock who fancies himself a bulletproof Lothario who doesn't give a damn about his object of desire other than to land her in the sack may totally disagree. And if that's the kind of mettle he's dealt, then good for him! A hallmark of a true Warlock is indeed to be strong and unflinching in times of crisis, but let's not kid ourselves. Most of us run on emotion because we're human. We get pissed off or elated, and whatever it is, we feel it deeply. Hell, passion is passion: We wouldn't be as horny as we are if we didn't get our balls twisted when things went wrong!

Not to imply the contemporary Warlock is any less manly than Anton LaVey's original followers. Those men proved their masculinity on many levels and reaped the real-world rewards for their achievement. And what was true 50 years ago still holds true today. You still have to walk the walk. Bravado aside, if you ain't cutting it by accomplishing something, all your macho posturing is just bullshit. Results set Warlocks apart from the herd. Eventually, kidding yourself and letting yourself off the hook for not giving something your all will negatively affect your overall persona, including your ability to seduce, as you'll learn later.

THE NEXT 50 YEARS WILL BE THE BEST

Warlocks have been using Satanism to navigate the world for more than five decades. These principles should be as much a part of the Warlock's psyche now as they were then. Warlocks must continue to embrace LaVey's time-tested methods and brilliant insights into the personalities of both men and women. The Satanic Warlock must not only embrace those ideas, but also understand their meaning at the deepest levels of his true self – his inner beast, demon, and god – and use these tools as a jumping off point. Today's more complicated and lightning-fast world requires us not to look for the quick fix (like the mainstream masses), but instead embrace those tools, combine them with deep thought about who and what the Warlock truly is, and then apply them to each individual Warlock's true Self.

This book defines the Warlock as he evolves from the end of the 20th century into the beginning of the 21st century. We see how he presents himself to the world, his tools to live life as a proper Warlock, and, most importantly, how he succeeds with the objects of his desire. As LaVey's *The Satanic Witch* presented a handbook of magical delights for women, *The Satanic Warlock* is a similarly devilish and diabolical working manual for success, forged from research and interviews with the last 50 years' best Satanic minds. This is no mainstream pick-up guide from Millennial "pants-on-the-ground" PUAs claiming they've found the secrets of seduction. Neither is it a one-note playbook from a random self-proclaimed "player." You won't find it next to the new Rachel Ray at your local Costco. This text burns with the light of real experience, applied Satanic principles, decades of tried and true se-duction techniques, proven psychological methodologies, and research culled from years of the author's formal study of human sexuality (as well as his "knocking around with the guys").

HOW TO READ THIS BOOK

For clarity, all references to a Warlock's desired sexual or romantic partner use the term "mate." After numerous discussions with Warlocks of all genders, the author has concluded that a male is a male. Males present the same desires and behaviors, regardless of sexual orientation. All instructions and advice regarding seduction and relationships apply to wooing a woman, another man, or both. Not to bore the reader with reams of scientific data, but what men want in the mating game is hardwired into their DNA: They are by nature anthropologically more promiscuous and inclined to "play the field." We may have cell phones, but we're still roaming cavemen, hunting for fresh food and fresh fucking. This is not to say men can't be monogamous, but all men of all genders – especially younger men with raging hormones – will hunt for sexual and ego (success) gratification. Men were designed to propagate the species and are out to have a blast (literally). As base, crude and blatantly, "wrong" as the politically correct herd might find that, nearly all men will agree with it. Those who don't are either outright lying or deep in denial.

Have you heard this one? That "women need to be in love to fuck … and men need to fuck to be in love?" Although this may sometimes be true, you'll learn this is not always the case. Women are in fact much more intelligent, calculating, and "opportunistic" when it comes to mate selection (more on this in the chapter on the Secret Art of Satanic Seduction).

Freud said people need love and work to be happy. Warlocks reading this book will use that principle and realize that Satanic men really only need two things to be happy: *Hunt and Prevail.*

A NOTE FOR THE GAY AND TRANSGENDER WARLOCK

As mentioned, the author conducted numerous discussions with Warlocks who define themselves sexually as other than "straight," leading to the conclusion that the needs of these Warlocks are best addressed in a separate volume. Although most of this book certainly applies to all Warlocks, myriad nuances, mating games, and dynamics have emerged within the LGBTQ communities, requiring and deserving specific attention.

The Gay Satanic Warlock will be written with a prominent gay Warlock. It will be a more focused and comprehensive approach to Warlocks of other sexual proclivities, but Warlocks of all stripes can still read, learn from, and enjoy this book. Many gay Warlocks participated in our research.

Magister Joe Netherworld weighs in:

"A companion book to *The Satanic Warlock* is a natural extension of the reality of Satanism itself. We all generate archetypes to help define and flesh out our self-created reality. Heroes and role models are missing from all modern constructs. In the scheme of Satanic imagery, everyone accepts the Villain as role model, but this is so much more important in the gay world.

Why? Because we must embrace the reality of the gay man's traditional social standing. We still live outside the norm, even in light of modern societal and governmental strides. There is compromise and a forced acceptance of 'normalcy' for the paltry rights granted. Real pressure is applied to conform. In response, gay Satanic men need a resource to bolster their outsider reality, not surrender it. Learn some lost and taboo history. Apply some arcane occult philosophy to your daily life. Give yourself an unfair advantage over the mundane world. Learn to enjoy your outsider status and use it to empower yourself.

In the great normalcy that is being preached to gay men, gay Satanic men must have a guidebook – a *Book of Homosexual Shadows* if you will – tailored to the Satanist who also identifies as a fully realized sodomite. We do not offer acceptance. We offer empowerment. Like tolerance, acceptance is a none too subtle act of control. We encourage the truth and the indulgence of your animal nature."

A NOTE FOR THE SATANIC WITCH

A number of our Satanic sisters may disagree with what is put forth in this book. They may shout "sexist" or "misogynist," especially when it comes to the rules of seduction. They may find the advice dated or think it doesn't apply, especially to those under the age of 30. They may feel it contradicts *The Satanic Witch*, thinking we've shifted the power to the male Satanist (we haven't – it's always been with the Witch, giving beauty to the mating dance). They may be put off by the blatant manipulation that is sometimes necessary in the game of love. Or they may simply disagree because they subscribe to their own customized, more politically correct (ugh) brand of Satanism. To them I politely say, read *The Satanic Bible* and *The Satanic Witch* – really read them. Satanists don't do political correctness. We respect and have opinions, but we don't forsake reason to spare someone else's misguided ideas of right and wrong or good and evil. This book lays out facts, regardless of how anyone *feels* about them.

What's more, this book is *for men*, so it may unapologetically refer to women as *broads, dames, tomatoes, hotties, chicks,* and/or some other classic (*skirt*? hubba hubba). This is how men talk, seldom when women are present, but nearly always in the company of other men. These are almost always terms of endearment and not meant to be derogatory, despite some feminist pushback.

In fact, Doktor LaVey was very fond of many of these terms. On one visit to his San Francisco Black House, he and I dined at one of his favorite local haunts. He was his natural flirty self, giving the hostess the business and using a few different names as we waited to be seated. LaVey knew I worked for men's magazines, looked at the hostess's legs and asked why girlie mags don't call them "gams," or why girls aren't "pieces of ass" anymore? I said maybe men want to be more literal these days and call good legs "good legs." He looked at me and said, "But where's the mystery in that? Where's the secret code? These magic words actually evoke their seductiveness." I could only nod in agreement.

Since I first began to notice the difference between men and women, which was somewhere around the time of my first birthday, women have sometimes been referred to as "broads, chicks, skirts, Baby, Honey and Sweetheart." A woman's reaction to those words depends a great deal on how they are spoken and in what context. To me, they are all ladies. - Frank Sinatra - *The Way You Wear Your Hat*

Of course this neo-feminist, PC man bashing doesn't apply to the glorious, beautiful, strong, and brilliant Witches who have helped make this book possible. They know they can always level the playing field with their inherent magic.

Want it straight from a seductive woman of real power who knows the Witch/Warlock dynamic like the back of her hand? Here's some sage advice from Magistra Ruth Waytz, with a note to the dubious Witch:

"You may hate me for saying it, but I like the 'Man's World' just fine, because that's where my magic works best. When women are in charge, everything quickly deteriorates into a clusterfuck of 'feelings' and divisiveness. Nobody will fuck a woman over like another woman. Show me three or more women and I will show you trouble. I've developed a different kind of magic entirely for women, but that's another story for another day....

The Satanic Witch is important (and still relevant) because it ignores political correctness (which has always been a lot of bullshit anyway) and just lays out the facts. Then it embraces and builds on those facts. Dr. [LaVey] was A MAN, writing to teach women how best to manipulate, take advantage, and otherwise vanquish him and his ilk – how to reduce even the scariest snarling wolf to a meekly purring kitten. Why do you think that is? Because this is a win-win situation.

Any woman who thinks she's harmed when a man calls her a broad, dame, chick (or a favorite of mine not mentioned, 'twist'), is completely loony. What you are CALLED means nothing; look at how you are being TREATED. Most, if not all, of these are terms of endearment and appreciation. Who doesn't want to be appreciated? A lot of thought and style went into those terms, which is why 'good legs' is such a thudding leaden replacement for 'gams.' And although LaVey was right to identify this as 'code,' it's far from secret.

Dr. is hardly discreet, and anyone finishing that book gets more than a casual familiarity with his personal and sometimes quite specialized fetishes. I am reminded of the line from Hitchcock's 'Vertigo' when an almost maniacal Jimmy Stewart takes Kim Novak shopping for THAT ONE GRAY SUIT and the saleslady says, 'Well, the gentleman certainly knows what he wants.'

Indeed he does. And it's ours for the taking, ladies, if we just pay attention and choose to play along. We are, of course, always free to give (or withhold) what we know they want. Therein lies the power, and the play.

And spare me that crap that 'we shouldn't have to' act or look or smell or move or whatever, just to please a man. 'Should' is the stupidest word in our language. 'Is' is far more valuable, in every circumstance. For my money, that's the Satanic perspective, male or female. I don't waste a lot of time crabbing about 'should' when 'is' gets results.

Am I a 'feminist?' I sure hope not. Am I pissed off that we've legalized gay marriage (hooray!) but still can't ratify the Equal Rights Amendment that passed IN THE 1970s??? Yeah. But do I hate men and see the war between the sexes as a battle to the death? Oh my, no.

You say a smart Witch will always level the playing field.

Level it? I NUKE IT."

And there it is – the opening act for Warlocks of all levels. But know this above all else: Satanism DOES NOT SUFFER poseurs, bullshitters, losers, or anyone else who just talks a good game. A true Warlock PRODUCES. Conversely, he does not – excuse the expression – *dick around*! In order to know yourself as a true Warlock and function as such in the world, you must prove your accomplishments in whatever field you choose. To be your own god, as Magus Gilmore says, a true "I-Theist," you must first hold close the dictum, "As above, so below."

So rejoice, Warlocks! You may not like or agree with what you find here, but this is the real deal, culled from (and tailored to) the Satanic man. You hold in your hands the only "wing man" you will ever need, the straight diabolical dope. Here is your infernal compass to victory – in the bedroom OR the boardroom!

WHAT IS A 21ST CENTURY WARLOCK?

"Walk the world on two legs; live as though you have four."

WHO IS THE WARLOCK?

Warlocks sealed their rightful pacts with the Devil when Anton Szandor LaVey founded the Church of Satan in 1966. He elevated them from "assistant witches" (barely more than helper monkeys in stale magical goddess worship) into equals of their Satanic sisters and sorcerers in their own right.

The Warlock has always identified with the beasts of the field while making his way in the world as magician, consummate seducer, tempter and irresistible, villain. The Warlock's lust for life is matched only by his innate affinity for the macabre and the pursuit of dark delights.

What's more, Satanism's timely emancipation of male Devils created the only lasting bulwark against the radical feminization of men that has unfortunately festered and shows little sign of slowing.

We know to recognize and celebrate the Warlock in all his power and grandeur! The Satanic man combines his primal instincts and learned behaviors, culled from the rewards of indulgence, the thrill of competition, and the occasional hard knock to the head. He is a breed like no other. Warlocks today are a unique ethnicity, reared on the teachings of LaVey and forged by decades of applied rational philosophy.

Most Warlocks (usually at the curious time of puberty) find resonance with the Satanic idea that we are, in fact, animals, albeit with brains that make us unique – our own gods – and often treacherous. Certainly we are suited for physical pleasure of many varieties. Research continues to find that men are much more prone to indulgence than women.

Now consider that one of the prime movers of human behavior (topping the list for most men) is to reproduce and propagate the species. Some snidely call this urge base, dangerous and uncivilized, when pursued for pleasure alone. But the carnal calling is woven into our male innards, sparking our every impulse and intention, despite claims to the contrary, most of which are made out of fear of reprisal or a sickening acquiescence to political correctness. This primal urge manifests as pleasure seeking, whether the target is fine food and drink, a lusted after item that brings joy, or a potential sexual mate. It is the celebration of the flesh and the Satanic way.

And I should know. At a very early age I happened to spy a small advertisement in one of my father's weekly magazines, touting films that were *"oooh la la,"* picturing a lovely raven-haired beauty whose black silk stockings peeked out from under her hiked-up skirt.

That was, no doubt, my initial ECI, and the first stirring of the hormones that would race through my young body (and continue to this day). I knew at that moment I wanted to share my titillation and joy for the unclad female with the rest of the world. I found an old briefcase, scribbled the words "The Ooooh La La, Company, Inc." across the front in black Magic Marker, and imagined an empire built on "nudie cuties."

That simple act revealed the urge that pushes and prods men like no other force in nature!

My magic "is-to-be" was born that day in my loins, and my empire (including *Old Nick* magazine) has brought me, dear fellows, the delights of many a nubile lass!

The Warlock also lives by the law of *Lex Talionis* (an eye for an eye), and believes it should be exercised regardless of flaccid societal rules and constipated political correctness that aim to steal his true power.

Satanists celebrate their inner black flame and label it appropriately. History puts us in good company: demons, seducers, scoundrels, magicians, sorcerers, gigolos, cads, lady-killers, voluptuaries, Casanovas,

Don Juans, rascals, rogues, and, yes, even our quintessential, yet maybe forgotten kin – the wolf.

Often characterized as a comical beast, the male wolf has long been the icon of woman-chasing and unbridled lust. What could be more appropriate and frankly, just plain fun, than to once again embrace this symbol? The Satanic Warlock walks with the beasts of the field, transforming himself from mere man to Satanic (Were) wolf – a man among beasts, "shearing the sheep" in magical lycanthropic fashion!

THE 21st CENTURY WARLOCK

We further the metaphor and say the Warlock identifies with the wolf in all its masculinity and cunning. This change from ordinary man to Warlock borrows from Anton LaVey's brilliant essay *How to Become a Werewolf: The Fundamentals of Lycanthropic Metamorphosis; Their Principles and Their Application.* One can easily understand the primal connection via an anthropomorphic label. As LaVey pointed out, the higher man uses his evolved ego (his inner Self) to metamorphose to his more animalistic nature. "He knows he is circumspect and cultured the greater part of his life. So transition to animalism can be entertained without compunction." The essay is a good mental backdrop, describing what can happen when man decides to turn himself into beast. Heightened feelings of fear, the thrill of pursuit, and sexual tension embody the wolf. These tools must be cultivated and mastered by the Warlock.

As that higher man, the Warlock uses Satanism to create a presence in the world unlike any other man. The Warlock changes from everyday human to a being, purely Satanic in thought and deed. Satanism provides the building blocks for his individual persona and is ultimately the key to what makes him unique.

We call this an *ethnicity*, rather than a traditional religion or philosophy, because the Satanic man identifies more with types than with individuals in a given group. We are more analogous to Vikings or pirates rather than simply "members of a church." We initiate and facilitate our metamorphosis through philosophy, but our transformation goes beyond mere thoughts and ideas.

Satanic men see the world differently. We abhor herd mentality and we consciously reject the fantasy belief in gods and religious dogma designed to entrap and enslave. We know that's for the rubes, and that none of it pays off in the end! We don't blindly adopt looks, styles, hobbies, or anything else to conform to pop culture "hipness." We don't want to be accepted anywhere if political correctness is required. Yes, we are rebellious in nature, but we don't don a worn-out rebel badge for pure shock value or to curry admiration. As Magus Peter H. Gilmore so aptly points out in *The Satanic Scriptures*, "We are not automatic contrarians, simply countering whatever is in widespread social fashion or might be prevalent in our vicinity." This is true. We aren't just naysayers; we know what we like (and don't like) and those who don't should be summarily dismissed!

Knowing that Warlocks are born not made sets the stage for all that follows. It mentally prepares us to answer the call; to cultivate and unleash the glorious revelation of the Satanic man lurking inside us since birth.

To this day, horror films, amusement park spook houses, cemeteries, old copies of *Famous Monsters of Filmland* and *Castle of Frankenstein* magazines, monster models and toys, and late-night TV binging on old Zacherley (the northeast's TV horror movie ghoul) are virtual comfort food for me in times of crisis, loneliness, boredom, or sheer melancholy.

Some call it weird, but Warlocks know that deep-seated desire motivates and soothes. I get a real thrill out of scaring the hell out of folks – especially the girls who scream with delight, sometimes peeing their pants. (Doktor LaVey loved me telling him these stories!)

One Halloween our gang rented an old mansion near a cemetery and threw a huge bash. We made the girls walk through the graveyard before entering the house. Of course, some of the boys were hiding behind the headstones or under leaves, waiting to jump out and scare the bejesus out of them.

I targeted one particular well-developed blonde I had my eye on and made sure I sprung out just as she passed. Not only did she pee her white panties, but she got so excited that she dragged me down into the pile of leaves, pulled down my zombie pants and begged me to give it to her, right there on hallowed ground!

We Warlocks knew from an early age that we didn't quite fit the standard definition of what a man is or how he should act. We identified with many different archetypes, role models, and people we admired. But something was always missing … an elusive, indescribable, yet omnipresent hunger in the belly. More importantly, we felt a dark presence; black flames illuminated our interest in the bizarre, the macabre, and the occult.

Embracing our dark aesthetic furthered our calling and built a home for our desires and pleasures. We devoured books, music, films, and art, developing our interests and finding our kindred. We discovered the deep-seated core of what made us unique. *The Satanic Bible* crystallized this revelation in our minds and awoke the demon within. This demon, born in our own pleasurable Hell, thumbs his nose at what society dictates. And now we unleash that Warlock Self upon the world.

THE NEW WARLOCK SELF

The 21st Century Warlock must embrace LaVey's description of "transmogrification," and by his own hand magically create his new Self, using the principles of LaVey's Personality Synthesizer to develop a new, more confident persona.

The Warlock must first have a solid grasp of the Synthesizer's "types" and the desires of the corresponding Majority and Demonic selves. Lack of awareness of those principles (not knowing where one fits on the Clock) leaves the Warlock unprepared to take the next steps to identifying his new and true Self. Creation of the new Self begins with the Clock.

Regardless of his "type," all weakness is not very Satanic, dilutes the overall persona, and is the death knell of confidence – a prime aspect of the true Warlock Self. The Warlock must exude strength, whatever his Majority Self may be. For example, a six o'clock Warlock may be somewhat feminine, longing for a dominant 12 o'clock woman. Even the slightest insecurity here creates complete failure, because without confidence he cannot successfully broadcast his Demonic Self to his intended mate. Again, regardless of your "type," security in that type must always be exhibited. All men are judged by their confidence.

The Warlock must take this knowledge to the next level and use it to create a newly powerful Warlock Self – melding the temporal and spiritual into a superior personality (based on a chosen Archetype, discussed in Chapter 2).

Unlike the Satanic Witch, who uses her witchy wiles to manipulate a world that unfortunately still shuns aggressive women, the Warlock must build upon his outward and immediately apparent core to create and bolster his image. Men are expected to be men. The Witch can often snare a man with her looks alone, but for Warlocks, *perception* is 90% of the game. If the outward Warlock Self – fueled by a strong belief in the inner Self – screams power, confidence and charisma, everything else will fall into place.

Most exemplary Warlocks have always consciously and subconsciously cultivated the Self, making it shine through and reflect their true Satanic position in the world. This inner strength radiates out and informs how the Warlock is perceived by others: how he conducts himself, how he reacts to circumstances, how he finds, chooses and seduces a mate, how he pursues his interests and career, how he enjoys the finer things in life, how he faces danger, and how he loves those closest to him.

For the fortunate few who are born with these innate abilities, the Warlock Self comes naturally. For the rest, it's a lifelong process of practice, trial and error, and fine-tuning until the dark knowledge becomes second nature. The Self creates a kind of muscle memory, making performance as a Warlock come naturally instead of as the result of conscious thought or effort. The Warlock Self will always be your guide. Habit will eventually take hold, regardless of whether it is inborn or learned.

With the aforementioned (Were)wolf metaphor as a model, we begin our own lycanthropic process, through which the Warlock (or aspiring Warlock) sheds his former self and takes up the powerful and ferocious Satanic mantle he always suspected he had. These inklings of being different and unique were catalysts, pushing the Warlock to Satanism in the first place, and they are incredibly potent tools. They live deep within the cells, sinews, and brain and become reignited when the Warlock finds his true Self and hears his ultimate Satanic calling. Don't ignore these signals – they come from your core and broadcast your true essence. This Warlock Self is the basis of all things to come – and dear fellows, it can be harnessed.

Herein lies the esoteric, practical, and researched knowledge to do just that – at your fingertips – for the first time in Satanic history!

Strip away all preconceived ideas of what you are, who you are, and who you want to be. The first step in creating the Warlock Self is akin to a Native American vision quest ritual where a brave would sit sleep-deprived in a small room or tent or walk alone for hours or days on end until he "saw" the man he was to become. This is not a phony New Age visualization technique; it is the basis of all meditation. Sensory deprivation and extreme physical stress often produce "visions." Sages, mystics, and occult practitioners have employed these techniques for centuries.

But unlike these practices, the Satanic man, by virtue of studying *The Satanic Bible* and *The Satanic Rituals* has the benefit of applying already codified, documented, and effective methods of ritual. Greater Magic can be used as the foundation to sharpen the Warlock's desired outcome. By concentrating on the specific type of Warlock he wants to be, the ritual will help him visualize and set the process in motion. (More on the Warlock Archetypes and creating the Warlock Self in following chapters.)

By using focus and intention, the Warlock simply and effectively keeps his Warlock Self in his mind – a mental picture, so to speak, of his ultimate persona. Rituals can be designed and customized to invoke the ideal Self. As LaVey said in *The Satanic Rituals*, "Modern Satanism realizes man's need for an 'other side,' and has realistically accepted that polarity – at least within the confines of the ritual chamber. Thus a Satanic chamber can serve – depending on the degree of embellishment and the extent of the acts within – as a chamber for the entertainment of unspoken thoughts, or a veritable place of perversity." This is not a new concept for the practicing Warlock, but an often overlooked method of changing one's Self. Chamber rituals are for the most part designed to achieve a material goal, which is perfectly acceptable. But in transforming the Warlock Self, the chamber and associated rituals should serve the Warlock as the portal for a mental and physical transformation as well.

Extrapolating the overall use of ritual allows it to be better understood as a tool to facilitate the making of the Warlock Self. We again see how Satanism, in its pure wisdom, has always been a step ahead! Satanic ceremonies – whatever they are – are designed to elevate us to god status without the nihilistic baggage. And there is no foundation better than the act of ritual and Greater Magic to begin the process.

If his desire and purpose are strong enough – regardless of mental and physical attributes – the Satanic Warlock will create a Self that far surpasses anything he could ever imagine. This new Self will *become the actual Warlock.* The outcome depends entirely on the amount and details of the Warlock's preparation and ceremony. For example, if the Warlock is a timid 98-pound weakling who longs to embrace the heavy metal aesthetic, he must prepare himself by outfitting his ritual chamber (wherever that may be) with stories, photos and films of this desired Archetype. The common practice of intense visualization of a desired outcome in tandem with the more potent reinforcement that one is, by nature, a Satanist is the prescription for transformation!

Of course this doesn't mean the pencil-necked geek will become a rock god overnight, but the constant mindset, identification and belief, in one's Self as that Archetype will eventually win out.

I had a realization during the building of my own ritual chamber. It suddenly occurred to me that I'd subconsciously styled it after a pictorial that ran in *Old Nick* magazine. As I performed the magic to create the space, I was visualizing my chosen "Gentleman" Archetype. The only thing that was missing were the candles000 and they were about to be delivered by UPS.

When the doorbell rang, I was pleasantly surprised to see a 30-something brown-uniformed female driver, package in hand. Although I was completely covered in dirt and disheveled from working on the subterranean chamber, I distinctly felt the mating call. The mere sight of her bountiful bosom straining her work shirt manifested the lust as was befitting my secret place. I knew it was time to summon my inner Archetype – my Sinatra, my Hefner, my Errol Flynn – and redouble their debauchery. I *needed* to seduce this gal. Fortunately my chamber must have evoked some dark curiosity in this girl as well, because she was clearly giving me the signal to make a move. As the image in mind became the Self I visualized, I got the courage (and the boner) to take advantage of the situation. Before I knew it, her body brushed against my hand, her blouse was unbuttoned, ... and let's just say the rest of her deliveries were very late that day.

WARLOCKS SPEAK OUT

Spanning decades of diabolical wisdom, experience, and in many cases, unmatched depth of knowledge about Satanism (and life), our brothers have searched the depths of their minds to define what they believe is the essence of the 21st century Warlock.

Our kind has always had: an ability to "read the mark;" independence; confidence; and a mastery of Lesser Magic. We have all employed sex, sentiment, and wonder to the fullest. And as all men, Warlocks are visual animals with an eye toward overall aesthetics (and a well-turned ankle of course). We are attuned to the finer things in life and have the ability to customize our worlds. The Warlock is a visionary, a hunter, a doer, and ALWAYS a Devilishly dashing gentleman.

To better illustrate the idea I share words from our own exemplary Warlocks, speaking on how they see the Satanic man, the power within, and more importantly how they keep their lives filled with success, carnal delight, and delicious indulgence.

A MASTER OF HIMSELF

The exemplary Warlock acknowledges the power within him and the forces around him that have come together to manifest the changes he demands and produce real results.

He is someone who possesses the needed skills, talents and attributes to be seductive, attractive, appealing, and successful. He is abundant in the resources needed to attain his desires. He overflows with Lesser Magic and successfully employs Greater Magic, yet has just the right amount of humility about it, knowing that over-inflated egos are the beginning of a Warlock's undoing. A Warlock is a man who has (and is) the entire package, knows it, and displays this fact in an enticing manner, never "trying too hard." If you have to try, you are not doing, and if you are not doing, you are not being, and if you are not being, you are not having, because to HAVE, one must DO!

An exemplary Warlock is an individual who is driven, passionate, loyal to his loved ones, eager to obtain his desires, brutally honest with himself, always aware of his turn-ons and turn-offs, has clearly defined standards, is willing to negotiate but never lowers his standards in the process, and always makes it a point to finish what he starts.

***

As a Warlock, I utilize Lesser Magic on a daily basis to influence personal interaction, succeed in business, and invade the minds of those whom I desire or condemn.

***

Real world success is the hallmark of an exemplary Warlock. You must define and achieve goals in life, never stopping. The goals are up to the individual but meeting them is the definition of success. You must own your aesthetic and positively represent Satanism through actions, not words.

***

The Satanic Warlock is a man who successfully shapes his total environment to derive a life of happiness.

Not only does he avoid self-deceit, but he has the discipline to master his own actions and thoughts, channeling them into the actions that create his desired outcomes.

***

He is smart and wise.

He is proud but not pretentious to the point of counter-productivity.

He can read people. He abhors solipsism. He does not stupidly assume that others share his perspective. Rather he observes. He listens.

He picks up on the subtle clues that reveal a person's desires, values, fears, and goals, even when they are not explicitly stated.

A MAGICIAN

He is a master of Lesser Magic. He lives by the Rules of the Earth. He embraces the Seven Deadly Sins to a level of happiness and indulgence without self-injury. He avoids the Nine Satanic Sins.

He can not only masterfully manipulate the general public, but manipulate the manipulator as well. He is one who can woo and charm his desires from even the strongest Magician. He sees what he wants out of life, knows that he can obtain anything he puts his mind to, and goes out and gets it.

He is capable of understanding history and applying it to the current situation in order to make a well-informed prediction of a likely future. This is a skill and is a great source of power. Indeed, it seems magical to the lesser men around him who see him use this skill. They are amazed at his ability to predict and anticipate events before they happen, and position himself accordingly for maximum advantage.

***

Manipulating those around him is a large part of what it means to be a Warlock, but it's not all it means. The Warlock title is a badge. Before he pins it on his chest, the Warlock must earn the title by having a passion for life.

He must interact with life, not simply brood in darkness as the world spins around him. A successful Warlock is alive and present in the world, sampling and appreciating its many treasures.

A REBEL

He is a non-conforming individualist, at least internally. He is an independent thinker and a discerning consumer of beauty and pleasure whose tastes are shaped little, if at all, by those of other people.

The exemplary Warlock has risen above "good and evil" and, while knowing how the world remains dominated by "unsane" guidelines that almost always guarantee an unhappy, unsuccessful life, he chooses to recognize that the desire for the rest of the world to "get it" is only a personal preference, not a demand. Consequently Warlocks tend to develop a high tolerance for frustration, knowing it is the secret ingredient in achieving almost any worthwhile success in life.

He is a man of broad vision. He is capable of seeing the big picture and the full strategic perspective. He probably plays chess and has the ability to think several moves ahead, both in the game on the board and in the game of life. He is mindful of past orthodoxies. He knows well the dictum that those who do not learn from history are doomed to repeat it.

The exemplary Warlock will therefore tend to be far more flexible in what he feels free to do, to try, and to challenge than most anyone he will ever meet. He is not bound by the need to please others, but he finds it pleasing when others meet his needs. He is no longer constrained by the need to achieve certain results, finding this allows him to get those results more easily. He increasingly tends to view the universe as a toolbox to use to build the future he desires, rather than a zoo in which he is trapped with crazy and irritating talking monkeys.

The Satanic Warlock successfully shapes his total environment to derive a life of happiness across a broad spectrum that includes but is not limited to sexuality. The Compleat/Satanic Witch *is a guide for women, instructing them on techniques for seducing and capturing men as a means of securing themselves a good life. Written from the perspective of the mid-20th century, it was spot on. At that time the primary mechanism for women to attain a life of happiness was to successfully attach themselves to the right man. Usually this meant to marry well. The Satanic Warlock, as a man, particularly a man of the 21st century, however, must approach life with a much more complex strategy. Obtaining the right mate or mates is an important, but by no means complete or even sufficient, mechanism for today's Satanic Warlock to attain a life of happiness. One must be able to attain both Power and Pleasure. Power includes wealth and knowledge and independence of action, free from the constraints of others. Pleasure may include the arrangement of one's life so as to attract desirable sexual partners, but may also (or alternatively) include attainment of other pleasures: sensual, aural, visual, and more.*

***

I read The Satanic Bible *in high school. Growing up, I was always an outcast and I figured there was something wrong with me. The treatment I got from my peers created such depression and anxiety that I genuinely believed I thought differently than anyone else on earth. Upon reading* The Satanic Bible *I realized that I truly was different, that I am a Satanist, and that it's okay to be an outcast. What a relief to know I don't have to try to fit in anymore. I can be myself without trying to be something else.*

A HUNTER

An exemplary Warlock is a seasoned hunter. Patient, calculating, and alert to the demands of his prey and surroundings.

He finds power in his cultivated talents, pleasure in as much of life as possible, and resonance with the archetypes that embody his nature.

The most important quality of an "exemplary Warlock" is to have progressed beyond "Phase One Satanism."

In Phase One it is common for many new Satanists to be outraged by the realities of a world in which most self-enhancing thoughts, feelings, and behaviors are rejected. They tend to want to "fix" the world while complaining about the same human nature that should be acknowledged and dismissed as "just human." The Phase One Satanist often gets stuck, demanding that reality should not be the way it is. With his newly-acquired insights into Satanic understanding he tends to focus on the "errors" around him and demand that non-Satanists change. This keeps him eternally frustrated and unnecessarily angry about things he has no direct control over.

Most human beings are trapped by the culture they live in. The Phase

One Satanist sees this and loudly protests. The exemplary Warlock sees the same world and leverages it to best benefit his own personal intentions.

And since it is often true that some of the most satisfying experiences come from the company of others one respects, the exemplary Warlock tends to form lasting relationships with these others. It is a trap to think you can only enjoy those who agree with you on everything. The exemplary Warlock recognizes this and decides to enjoy those individuals who contribute to his world and to reduce unnecessary contact with those who do not. He can get along with almost anyone, but doesn't need to!

Without a doubt, self-awareness is the core of a successful Warlock. Obviously an honest self-appraisal is useful in all facets of life, but it is most crucial to the Lesser Magic of a Warlock. Being adventurous enough to become the aggressor only has worth if he is able to deliver on promised offers. One guaranteed formula for failure is to offer something you knowingly cannot accomplish – the essence of pretension. A failed promise creates a feeling of disappointment that does not subside quickly (and Witches trade notes).

A RISK TAKER

Fire is wild and playing with it can either burn the house down or create spectacular thrills. Such is the risk, but it is only in risk-taking that big payouts are possible. Warlocks can never mitigate that idea entirely. They can, however, take necessary precautions simply by being able to see where realistic boundaries lay.

An exemplary Warlock experiences success, whatever this may mean to the individual as defined by the individual. Satanism has provided us numerous tools to achieve our respective goals and when these are coupled with applied logic (given the circumstance) and desire of intent, the rewards are almost inevitable. A Warlock should either be a success, or be extremely busy working to achieve that end.

A GENTLEMAN

An exemplary Warlock should be a respectful gentleman who is well versed in Satanic literature and can speak articulately about the Satanic philosophy. Like his female counterpart, the Warlock should possess an adept understanding of Lesser Magic and should be able to apply it skillfully, utilizing his best assets to accumulate victories in his daily life.

He is someone who is able to truly manifest the situations he desires. One who is healthy in body and mind and always one step ahead of the game.

He is confident, socially gracious man, who is not boisterous but generally "laid back," able to converse with people of diverse backgrounds and interests. He possesses a strong yet subtle sexual energy.

He is an individual with a unique sense of pride in all aspects of himself including aesthetics and choice of dress and conduct in the real world (along with the virtual one) and the ability to embrace his own faults as well as live life in parallel with them while learning from them.

He is an aesthete. He has style. He has good taste. He knows art and the basics of design. This allows him to find and surround himself with beauty. Men are visual animals. The eyes are the gateways to pleasure. The Warlock knows this and actively cultivates pleasure by surrounding himself with beauty, and through his patronage or his own creation, expands it into his broader environment and universe.

***

These are the words of real Warlocks who have shucked off the commonplace and mundane to enjoy the delights of darkness.

It is your quest – no, your duty – as a true man to fulfill your Satanic destiny and calling. Call forth your Hellish demeanor so you may enjoy all of the pleasures of the flesh *here and now!*

Thankfully, not only the Warlocks themselves understand who the Warlock is; several sister Witches were also interviewed for this book.

FROM SATANIC WITCHES

Magistra Blanche Barton's description of a Warlock:

A Satanic Warlock is a man who understands human needs and nature, and who positions himself, using that knowledge, to achieve his earthly goals. Applying principles of both Greater and Lesser Magic, humor, creativity, physical and intellectual prowess, ideal timing, self-awareness along with constant reflection and fine-tuning, he works for the betterment of himself and those he loves.

Other prominent Witches:

A man who is successful in his life by his own doing. A creator who forges his own path. Who takes pain and failures and transforms them into fuel for success. An individual who does not bow to anyone, but is unboastful, kind hearted, and always in search of knowledge.

***

A Satanic Warlock is one who is true to himself, above and beyond all other influences. He is comfortable in his own skin, confident in his abilities, classy in demeanor and an old fashioned gentleman.

***

I define a Warlock as a man who embraces and maximizes his ability to manipulate the world to his satisfaction. A man who knows how to cultivate and wield his power. Naturally, a Satanic Warlock is a man who does all this in accordance with what I define as the Satanic philosophy.

***

I have often equated the exemplary Satanic Warlock to Abraham Maslow's "Self-Actualized Man." If a self-actualized man walked into a party dressed for the beach and everyone else was in black tie, he wouldn't notice. Some might argue that one should never show up at a black tie affair unprepared. Going with this same analogy, however, I could totally see my husband, who is an exemplary Satanic Warlock and, well, most any Warlock I know, finding himself in a position where he ends up at a black tie affair in a Hawaiian shirt and Bermuda shorts, sauntering up to the bar like he owns the place, ordering a drink and flirting with the person next to him without batting an eye. So yes, a Satanic Warlock, to me, is very much a self-actualized man.

***

I'd say he has to have a good understanding of human nature, sexuality, and what motivates people, and be able to use that knowledge to his advantage. Most importantly, he has to be actively applying this knowledge, using it to better himself and reach his goals.

***

A Satanic Warlock is a gentleman. He is inherently intelligent, well mannered, trustworthy and sensitive, to his environment and those within it. He is charming and debonair. He takes on a style that matches his personality type, so therefore he can pull it off. To do this, he must have great self-knowledge and the ego to self-analyze.

So listen up, Warlocks! Snap out of your confused mindset that meanders about who and what you are. You inherently know you are unique because you've chosen the Left Hand Path and embraced Satanism. The seeds have been sown. Your transformation to a new (Were)wolf began the moment you realized Satanism resonated in every fiber of your being. Now it's simply a matter of honing your true Warlock Self, developing your inner magic, and demonstrating in every waking moment that you are a Satanic Warlock – a unique, intriguing, mysterious, fascinating, and sometimes dangerous man.

warlock wisdom

- He understands and lives the tenets of *The Satanic Bible.*
- He walks on two legs, but lives as though he has four.
- He embraces his dark inner Self.
- He knows he is part of an ethnicity rather than a "congregation."
- He is master of himself and is self-confident in all endeavors.
- He believes he is a god of his own making.
- He denies political correctness, trends and flaccid societal rules, living by his own code.
- He is dangerous when crossed, loving when loved.
- He is a gentleman.
- He is a magician.
- He is a hunter.
- He is a risk-taker.

CHAPTER TWO

WARLOCK ARCHETYPES

"Know The Devil Within."

For most people outside our circle, the word "witch" conjures images of scary Halloween cartoons, mysterious seductresses, or non-threatening "good witches" from TV shows like "Bewitched" and "I Dream of Jeannie." History and literature are rich with examples, both good and bad. But the Warlock has historically been little more than an afterthought – a mere "boy witch" – instead of how we see him: a true master of the dark arts. Most male Satanists take this slight seriously, particularly since nothing could be farther from the truth.

We are the embodiment of Satan himself! We have the power to morph, shape-shift, and present ourselves any way we see fit, seizing power over our environment and those we wish to seduce.

On a trip to Salem Massachusetts in the mid-1990s, accompanied by a lovely Goth girl who was a self-proclaimed witch of no particular discipline (although her Satanic skills certainly were evident in bed), the power of the Archetype crystallized in my mind. Despite a wonderful time "ghost hunting" in a city that bills itself as the occult capital of the country, some of the locals took issue with the shirt I was wearing (emblazoned with our Church Baphomet). The scene got particularly heated when a few dimwitted barflies decided that anyone "Satanic" was not welcome in what I later found out was a Wiccans Only watering hole.

As a number of the creeps razzed my date and me. I decided to teach them some good ol' Real Devil magic! I took the gents aside and bet them a night of drink that I could convince two of the girls in their

. . . . ✦ . ✦ . ✦ . ✦ . ✦ ✦ ✦ . ✦ . ✦ . ✦ . . . ✦ . . .
19

group to leave with me and my girl. The jerks jumped at the bet and were sure I could never pull it off. But what they didn't know was what I observed beforehand: One of their girls was eyeing my girl's ample rack intently. All I needed to do was sway her pal, which was actually a favor considering the douchebag she was shackled to. I charmed her with tales of romance and how a Satanic gentleman Warlock treats a woman in and out of bed. For one evening, I promised, she could escape into a world of her darkest desires. At the same time, my girl was touchy/feely with the wandering-eyed lesbian.

As you can guess, the girls quickly became part of our weekend entourage, leaving the sad Wicca wanna-boys holding their dicks in their hands.

Your challenge is to seize on situations like these and shine as an exemplary Warlock – to "know your devil" intimately and use your Satanic powers to forever banish the misconceptions surrounding who and what a true Warlock is. Many already know their strengths and have a strong foundation. But if it's time to forge a new Warlock Self – the basis for all your diabolic attributes (both physical and mental) – read on. You must be ready to brand yourself, so to speak, as a unique, mysterious individual... devilishly irresistible!

Anyone with whom our religion resonates will recognize the Archetype descriptions here as the foundations of all that is to come. They are the costumes, the special effects, the icing on the cake, and "The Sizzle Not The Steak". (to quote legendary advertising master David Ogilvy) Your Archetype identifies you as a particular Warlock, differentiating you from the world around you. It also helps crystallize your inner Demon, which is the engine that drives who you are and what you do. This secret power is your inspiration; the magic spell you cast over everyone you meet.

The following Archetypes are the product of interviews and observations with accomplished Warlocks and are the first step in creating your Warlock Self. They catalog some general qualities of many Warlocks, but they are not "absolutes." A plethera of information has been gathered over more than four decades through formal interviews, casual conversation, and real-world observation. The subjects were observed in action, showing how their outward style, appearance, and demeanor *created* the way they were perceived by others. And that is absolutely the key – perception! As already mentioned, a Warlock's standing in the world (and his attractiveness to a potential mate) is based 90 percent on perception. And perception is not the same as "looks." Warlocks who transform themselves into Satanic (Were)wolves fine-tune their personas and move forward in whatever "skins" they project.

Because we are visual animals, most men incorrectly assume women evaluate potential mates using our same criteria. A man sees a woman and scans her entire physical (i.e. sexually enticing) package, looking for something to trigger his mating response. If one woman doesn't *look* appealing (whatever speaks to his particular ECI or fetish), a Warlock will quickly move on to another. Conversely, women may certainly notice physical attraction, but they base their thumbs up or *thumbs down* on many other criteria, including humor, attitude, specific body parts (eyes, hands, hair), confidence, clothing, or occupation. And let's not forget money. Women, anthropologically speaking, are far more selective in choosing mates (yes, they're smarter about it and in it for the long haul) and are primarily "nesters" who want the best environment to nurture offspring. Men are geared to hunt, provide, wander, and have sex with as many women as possible in order to propagate the species. Feminists want us to believe we can force ourselves to "evolve" past this, but facts are facts. Evolution has been at it for millions of years and we still have gall bladders and pinkie toes.

A beautiful woman will always get me to ramp up my game. With a well-tailored suit, a smart cologne, steel bracelet watch, and my Archetype held close in my mind, I once made love to a woman so gorgeous my detractors would certainly say she was out of my league. I was one of many Warlocks at an historic Satanic gathering, and we were all eager to meet this woman. She was a model and one of the most attractive women ever to join the Church. The playing field was level, and many good-looking and accomplished men buzzed around this lovely creature, like starving bees in a patch of clover. I played my chosen Archetype to the hilt, picturing our night of passion as I listened to her talk, all the while really knowing and *believing* my Devil would win out.

I was pleased to be invited back to her room after the evening's festivities, expecting no more than a serious bout of flirting. She made herself comfortable, slipping out of her dress and into very little while I poured a glass of wine. After some light conversation I told her I really liked her (and boy did I!), but it was getting late and I should leave. I never verbally said I wanted to stay, but what I said and did as *my Archetype* sealed the deal. I confidently kissed her lightly on the lips and said, "Goodnight." I followed it up with, "But before I go…" as I slipped off her panties. She found her way to the bed and I spread her thighs, pleasuring her silky softness for many hours.

On that night (and many others) I proved the Warlock's *actual* physical attributes are almost irrelevant. Once he embraces his chosen archetype, everything about him can be designed and molded to project anything he believes he is – his true Warlock Self!

Worth repeating – the Warlock's actual physical attributes take a back seat to the Self he projects to the world. Once you commit to living your Archetype, the world really is your oyster!

So whether you consider yourself a scoundrel, a smooth seducer, a wily magician, or just a run-of-the-mill Satanist – at least one of the Archetypes here should ring a bell. If you don't find yourself entirely in one, feel free to craft your Warlock Self using anything and everything that speaks to your innermost Demon.

Which brings us to another key element in creating the Warlock Self; the ability to be a chameleon. As Satanists, we create our chosen reality and alter it to suit our needs. You may at first see yourself as *only* the Black Musician. But you have options, so why limit yourself? You'll have a wider field from which to select your object of desire. Businessman by day can become Romantic Rake (or other persona) after hours, just by changing outfits and accessories. Lesser Magic comes naturally when the Warlock Self is deftly appointed.

A list of popular celebrities and notable figures (iconic examples, both fictional and real) follow the Archetype descriptions to better illustrate each Warlock type. Each of these icons has been chosen for a particular appeal, and although we never divulge the names of our members without permission, all of these are considered de facto Satanists. The Warlock should study his icons in depth. See every film, read every book, drill down into the details of the person or the character and really *become* that person. Know his mannerisms, habits, speech patterns, and catch phrases until his persona is indistinguishable from your own.

A list of infernal names is also supplied for your edification and enjoyment. Many Warlocks find changing or augmenting their names helpful in immersing themselves in their new personas. A self-proclaimed Warlock often finds a touch of exoticism will enhance how he is perceived – but beware of what could be viewed as comical. Malcolm Cagliostro might get a sly wink and an invitation upstairs to see her etchings, while Damien Demogorgon is left to a night of "self-satisfaction."

First, perform this simple magical exercise: Close your eyes and quickly snap a mental picture of yourself. Don't give it any thought – just capture the image. What do you look like? Where are you? What are you wearing? Are you doing something? These are the primary elements of your Satanic Archetype. If none of the archetypes here matches your image, examine each one. Pick and choose as you see fit, crafting your own unique Warlock Self.

THE PRIMARY SATANIC WARLOCK ARCHETYPES

THE DEVILISH GENTLEMAN

A man of manners, refinement, and Devilish charisma, this Warlock is an epicurean, a hedonist, and a polished voluptuary. He is intelligent by worldly standards and possesses chameleon-like social capabilities. Not always classically handsome, but always outstandingly attractive, thanks to his deliberate, impeccable "look" that radiates class and sophistication. This Warlock may manifest his specific style as a reflection of his love for a particular time period or interest, like a 1940s gentleman or a mid-1960s jet-setting international playboy. His key appeal is cool confidence and the way he carries himself. He is absolutely comfortable in every scenario and it shows.

ICONIC EXAMPLES

James Bond
Christopher Lee
Frank Sinatra and The Rat Pack (Dean Martin, Sammy Davis Jr., Peter Lawford)
Hugh Hefner
Humphrey Bogart
Cary Grant
Desi Arnaz
Idris Elba
Vincent Price
Ian McShane
Al Pacino as John Milton, Esq. in "The Devil's Advocate" and Michael Corleone in "The Godfather"
Jack Nicholson
Morgan Freeman
Hannibal Lecter (as portrayed by Anthony Hopkins)
The Dos Equis "Most Interesting Man in the World"
Samuel L. Jackson

THE ROMANTIC RAKE

A poet, dreamer, or libertine, he is usually gifted with storybook good looks. This Warlock walks the line between feminine and masculine, but is never seen as anything less than totally attractive by all admirers. Often stylish and rebellious by contemporary standards, his mannerisms are gentile with a quiet calm. His look may border on androgynous at times, playing the Byronic seducer or swashbuckling pirate. Extreme Warlocks of this type flirt with being a bit of a fop, or act shy and retiring, but always with a Devilish twinkle in the eye. Many are musicians and actors, often labeled as notorious "bad boys."

ICONIC EXAMPLES

Johnny Depp
Errol Flynn
Sebastian Bach
Keith Richards
Charlie Sheen
Oscar Wilde
Nick Cave
Steven Tyler
Tim Curry as Dr. Frank N. Furter ("Rocky Horror Picture Show")
Mick Jagger
Adam Ant
Jim Morrison
The Vampire Lestat de Lioncourt ("Interview With A Vampire")
David Bowie
Liberace
The Scarlet Pimpernel
Prince

THE BLACK MUSICIAN

Either a professional musician or one who deeply identifies with the heavy and death metal culture, this Warlock is high on testosterone. He is aggressive, opinionated, and a staunch defender of Satanic principles, especially *Lex Talionis*. He expresses his style through an almost exclusively black wardrobe of warrior gear, leather, or other outrageous costuming. There is a likelihood he is into BDSM. He wears his hair long if possible and favors motorcycles (the louder the better) and extreme sports cars. His musical tastes may go beyond metal, but metal is his first love. Most Black Musician Warlocks have prominent tattoos of an infernal nature, signifying their celebration of their dark side and their disregard for the opinions of the squeamish.

ICONIC EXAMPLES

Nikki Sixx
Dee Snider
David Vincent
Rob Halford (Judas Priest)
James Hetfield (Metallica)
Peter Steele (Type O Negative)
Lemmy Kilmister (Motörhead)
Gene Simmons (KISS)
Ozzy Osbourne (with and without Black Sabbath)

THE OCCULTIST

The Occultist Warlock is an expert in the dark arts and a practitioner of ritual. He is often a scholar, specializing in the occult, the paranormal, and the esoteric arts. He does not believe in the myriad theories and "magickal" workings of traditional occultism, but he is aware of their meanings and impact on those who embrace them, seeking whatever power their mastery can impart to him. He may earn his living as a mentalist, shaman, astrologer, writer, or psychic investigator. This Warlock enrobes himself in the powers of explicit Satanic Magic and is never seen without his (usually black) costume and appropriate accessories, talismans, and sigils.

ICONIC EXAMPLES

Anton Szandor LaVey
John Dee
Harry Houdini
Bela Lugosi (in many of his roles)
Austin Osman Spare
H.R. Giger
Hjalmar Poelzig (Boris Karloff in "The Black Cat")
Dr. Strange
Svengali
Nostradamus
Severus Snape ("Harry Potter")
Faust
Alessandro Cagliostro (née Giuseppe Balsamo)
Saruman ("Lord of the Rings")
Sir Isaac Newton
Jack Parsons
Robert Anton Wilson
Max Maven

THE INTELLECTUAL

A scholar, deep thinker, philosopher, strategist, and academic, the Intellectual Warlock prides himself on fully understanding whatever subjects spark his interest. He knows the devil is in the *details*, and spends countless hours deep in study. He is the master of debate, remaining open-minded while arguing his points brilliantly. There is no typical "look" for this Archetype, but he is often labeled "brainiac" or "nerd." He may lack the flamboyance of the other Archetypes, but he almost certainly has a masterful grasp of the Satanic philosophy and can expound in great detail, often to his detractors' exhaustion.

ICONIC EXAMPLES

Sherlock Holmes
Wolfgang Amadeus Mozart
Niccolò Machiavelli
Ludwig van Beethoven
Victor Frankenstein
Egon Spengler (Harold Ramis in "Ghostbusters")
Neil deGrasse Tyson
Christopher Hitchens
Jeff Goldblum
The Doctor (From Doctor Who)
Joseph Campbell
Benjamin Franklin
Stephen Hawking
Socrates
Aristotle
Professor X(avier) ("X-Men")
Tony Stark ("Iron Man")

THE CREATIVE

This Warlock lives for his creations, whether they be artistic, commercial, or purely intellectual. Always on the fringe and always exhibiting a certain amount of flair, the Creative Warlock often chooses his passion over all else, including interpersonal relationships. He may enjoy a good party (especially in his honor), but he may also lock himself away at work for weeks or months on end. His burning need to bring his ideas to life and his ability to focus and immerse himself in whatever he undertakes make him dynamic and irresistible. Creative Warlocks change the world, a concept best illustrated by example.

ICONIC EXAMPLES

Steve Jobs
Béla Bartók
Bob Dylan
Richard Wagner
Frederick Douglass
Salvador Dalí
Frank Lloyd Wright
Willy Wonka
Leonard Bernstein
Mark Twain
Langston Hughes
Stanley Kubrick
Pablo Picasso
Andy Warhol
Charles Eames
Hunter S. Thompson
Elvis Presley

THE EVERYMAN

A Warlock with no distinct characteristic other than his deep and passionate understanding and projection of Satanic philosophy. His average looks may not conjure the word "gorgeous," but his strong intellect, personality, and sense of humor transcend the physical. He is "Everyman" because he seduces those attracted to him with his genuine interest and expertise in the subjects he loves – film, music, comic books, novels, fantasy, architecture, or the arts. He is the Warlock no one ever sees coming. He prevails in career and love (sometimes over higher-profile Warlocks) because he works harder and pays close attention to what will win his intended. Because he can't rely on his outward appearance, he brings his A-game and appeals exclusively to women's non-visual criteria. Warlocks who think the Everyman is a less desirable Archetype would be well served to reconsider: His ability to approach any woman means he has the largest group of potential mates.

The Everyman is also a stand-up guy who can deliver the goods. (He may even be a UPS or FedEx man!) Often, as a "blue collar" worker, his occupation might require him to wear a uniform. Fireman, security officer, policeman, soldier, chef, lineman, construction worker, sailor, airline pilot – the garb shows you are rock solid and an expert at handling real world situations. You can take the heat, and are the go-to guy for a job that has training beyond what most people understand. Uniforms have always had sex appeal, and when you roll up your sleeves and get to work, if the lady you want to impress sees a Baphomet or Brimstone sigil tattooed on your brawny forearm, that might just seal the deal.

These fellas have traditional masculine archetypal occupations, so maleness is explicit and then enhanced by subtly adding the Satanic as the underlying secret of these man's men. Adding the exoticism of Devilish underpinnings to what are otherwise more common, earthy looks, brings power by contrast. You are not "just" what the outfit denotes: you are also a Warlock.

A word about the "Dad Bod" phenomenon:

In a 2015 article for The Odyssey Online, Mackenzie Pearson writes

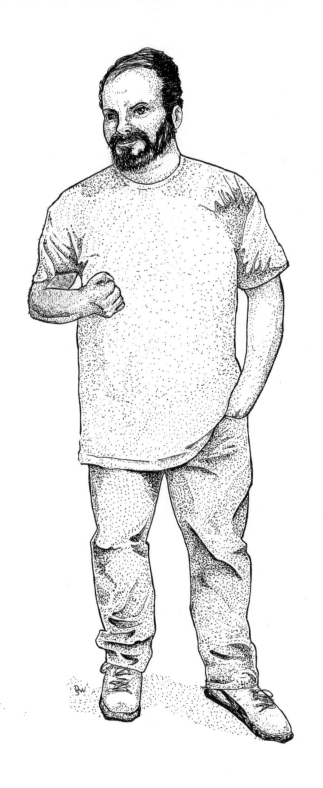

an excellent and insightful article about the "dad bod."

"The dad bod is a new trend and fraternity boys everywhere seem to be rejoicing. Turns out skipping the gym for a few brews last Thursday after class turned out in their favor. While we all love a sculpted guy, there is just something about the dad bod that makes boys seem more human, natural, and attractive."

She makes a good point! And it's not just about the man. Pearson reminds men that women "like being the pretty one," and that super-fit men often trigger their own insecurities about body image. Women also like to picture their future together with their men almost immediately after meeting them. Pearson adds, "If he already has the dad bod going on, we can get used to it before we date him, marry him, have three kids with him. We know what we are getting into when he's got the same exact body at the age of 22 that he's going to have at 45."

But not everybody is a fan.

Brian Moylan's Time Online article says, "A man is perfectly fine if he's sweet, cuddly, and a good provider. Meanwhile, the female equivalent of the Dad Bod is an acronym not fit for publication on a family website, starting with "mom I'd like to…" (You know the rest.) While a man is valued for his warm and fuzzy demeanor, a woman is valued only as a sexual object. And the women in question don't look like they've ever entered an all-you-can-eat Buffalo Wing contest like their Dad Bod brethren."

Pearson may celebrate women being "the pretty ones," but Moylan thinks that just reinforces destructive stereotypes. He says, "The Dad Bod continues to reinforce inequality about what is acceptable for men and women. While the ladies have to go to Pilates and watch every single calorie, guys are free to let themselves get lazy, chow down on all the chips and guac they want, and still expect their prospective mates to be fit."

ICONIC EXAMPLES

Jack Black
Ernest Borgnine

Zach Galifianakis
Patton Oswalt ("King of Queens")
Jerry Seinfeld
Chris Rock
Seth Rogen
John Belushi
Louis C.K.
Ron Swanson ("Parks and Recreation")
Steve Carell
Drew Brees
Forrest Whitaker
Carl Reiner
Sam Simon

INFERNAL NAMES

Part of the Warlock's chosen Archetype could also include add-ing to or changing his name to appear more Devilish and mysterious, particularly if he chooses a lesser-known infernal name. Words are pow-erful, and a unique name can help people remember you more easily and identify you as a magician. Unique names like *Corvus, Draconis, Storm*, or the title of *Count*, for example, create a lasting image and set you apart from the mundane Joes, Jimmys and Bobs of the everyday world. An exotic name also helps in your own Lesser Magic as a constant reminder to maintain your self-image. Introducing yourself as Ahriman instead of Alan makes all the difference in those critical first moments.

A word of caution: don't get too hokey. *Yan-gant-y-tan* is hard to spell and pronounce, and people might expect you to change into a bat (or swallow your tongue) when you utter it. You want to be interesting and memorable, not ridiculous and easily dismissed. More *Hmmm*, less *Jesus! Really?* Choose something arcane or create your own portman-teau of interesting words.

Following are some traditional occult and demonic names that can be adopted or modified to reflect your chosen Archetype. An add-ed benefit of researching the infernal name you take is you have an instant and compelling story should anyone ask, "Where did you get that interesting name?"

Abaddon	Bile
Abigor	Buer
Abraxas	
Adramelech	Cali
Aguares	Carnivean
Ahpuch	Carreau
Ahriman	Caym
Alastar	Cerbere
Alocer	Chemosh
Amduscias	Cimeries
Amon	Coyote
Andras	Crocell/Procell
Apollyon	Dagon
Asmodee (Asmodeus)	Damballa
Astaroth	Demogorgon
Azazel	Deumus
	Diabolus
Baalberith	Dolemite
Bael	Dommiel
Balan	Dracula
Balaam	Dumah
Baphomet	
Barbatos	Emmo-O
Barsinister	Eurynome (Euronymous)
Behemoth	
Beherit	Fenriz
Belial	Flaga
Beleth	Fleegle
Belphegor	Forcas
Belzebuth (Beelzebub)	
Berith	Garuda
Beyrevra	Gomory

Gorgo
Gozer
Gressil

Haborym
Harumph
Haurus
Hornblas
Hecubus
Hockstetter
Hungadunga

Immodium
Ipes

Jambi
Jub-Jub

Kobal

Lechies
Leviathan
Lieberman
Loki
Lucifer

Malphas
Mammon
Mantus
Marchocias
Marduk
Mastema
Melchom
Melek Taus
Mephistopheles

Moloch
Mictian
Milcom
Minos
Misroch
Moloch
Mormo
Mycale

Nergal
Nickar or Nick
Nihasa
Nija
Nybbas
Nyuck
Olivier
Orabas

Paimon
Pan
Paymon
Picollus
Pluto
Pokemon

Pruflas
Rahouart
Ribesal
Ronwe

Sabazios
Sammael
Samnu
Schtupp
Scox

Sedit
Sekhmet
Set
Shaitan
Shiva
Stolas
Szandor

T'an-mo
Tap
Thamuz
Thith
Typhon

Ukobach

Verrier
Volac

Xaphan

Yaotzin
Yan-gant-y-tan
Yen-lo-Wang

Zaebos
Zuul

warlock wisdom

- Identify your Archetype – "Know Your Devil."

- Satanic Archetypes are not cast in stone and are a composite of many common Warlock characteristics.

- Archetypes are designed to help identify your strongest aspects.

- Archetypes are not meant to create a false self, but rather to enhance and distill your ideal Warlock Self.

- Using an Archetype in Greater Magic can assist you in identifying and strengthening your natural persona.

- Adopting an exotic Infernal name can add to your mystery and help you remember to project your Warlock Self.

CREATING THE WARLOCK SELF

"Become Gods Among Men."

There's never been any such thing as "warlockcraft." Warlocks have historically been lumped in with witches and witchcraft, or in Wiccan circles, as assistants in the workings of the great magical mother. Satanism's liberation of the individual ended all that and gave Warlocks the equal standing they deserve as sorcerers and seducers – not also-ran magical eunuchs.

So let's define the Warlock's true Self – the inner Demon that drives the Satanic man in everything he says and does.

In *The Satanic Witch*, Anton LaVey wrote that one can tell a book by its cover and, when using witchery, a woman must appeal to a man's second layer, his Minority Self that hungers for what he lacks in his everyday life. She will play whatever part is required to get what she wants from her target.

A codified equivalent or rulebook for Satanic men never appeared because it was accepted as fact that men didn't need help. They could get what they wanted, whoever they were and however they looked or acted. That may be true for a gifted minority, but that kind of thinking has led to a number of Warlocks not living up to their potential as exemplary Satanic men. It's also prompted some less satisfied Warlocks to envy their more accomplished Satanic brothers and wonder why they're always "out in the cold."

We've established that men are primarily visual and that Witches have it a little easier because of it. They quickly determine what men want to see, and (thanks to *The Satanic Witch*) they know how to use what they've got to bewitch their chosen man. But we know women want more than just looks, so men cannot rely on looks alone to win the mating game. In most cases of seduction, good looks without substance will actually be a detriment.

We must build upon LaVey's analysis and adoption of photographer William Mortensen's *Command to Look*. LaVey wrote, "Learning to effectively utilize the command to look is an integral part of a witch's or warlock's training. To manipulate a person, you must first be able to attract and hold his attention. The three methods by which the command to look can be accomplished are the utilization of sex, sentiment and wonder, or any combination of these."

Sage words indeed, but this technique is only one part of the Warlock's persona and Archetype. A Warlock's training to master his new Self must not only employ the thematic elements of visual appeal, but must also surpass those tactics and cement his new inner being. He needs a combination of a more powerful outer image and the inner confidence to project it.

Satanists don't delude themselves. Before he can make any changes, a Warlock must be brutally honest in assessing his strengths and weaknesses. If he's short, fat, never showers, doesn't own a nose hair trimmer, and wears only sweat pants, the Devilish Gentleman Archetype is going to be a challenge (to say the least). This is not to say it's impossible, but he must make a lot of changes to build a Self that exudes enough of that Archetype to draw attention away from the shortcomings he can't change. Once he honestly evaluates how much work is needed to create his chosen Archetype, he can begin creating his new Self.

The Warlock inherently knows he is a truly diabolic man, and can be whoever he wants to be. This is his great strength. He's realistic about what he can't change, but he also knows the power of illusion. Since this book is primarily for men who choose a female target, our Warlocks must learn to move away from the purely visual criteria and go deeper when constructing the Warlock Self.

TRADE THE SIX-PACK FOR THE 666-PACK

Most women, bless their black hearts, won't immediately disqualify a man who doesn't sport a six-pack washboard stomach. Sure it helps – especially with younger women (teens and 20') – but as a woman matures, her criteria for selecting a (bed) mate become more sophisticated and geared toward confidence, kindness, and the ability to protect the home and father healthy children. Worried about that gut? Studies show that most heterosexual women don't look there: They are checking out eyes, hands and butts, and finally hair. A man's overall body type is far down on the priority list – a beacon of hope for Warlocks who've embraced the dad bod and either can't or won't spend a quarter of their waking hours pumping iron.

Women are acutely attentive to many more signs and subliminal messages than are obvious and on the surface. They also have their own ECI and subconscious fetishes. In many ways they're not even aware of what's happening, as their particular hardwiring makes unconscious biological and sociological decisions. Many a Witch interviewed for this book has said that she may have eyed an attractive guy and allowed him to approach her, only to dump his sorry ass when he opened his mouth and blurted out something stupid or was immediately nailed as a fraud. Her inner compass kicks in fast, often overruling her initial attraction to appearance.

I'm often shocked by how much tail some of my friends get. They aren't classically handsome; they truly embody the Everyman Archetype. They are different from each other, but they all employ a combination of pure confidence, humor, and depth that goes beyond the surface.

One of my co-workers at *High Society* magazine was swarthy, very short, a bit paunchy, and at best average looking, but boy did he have *a way with women.* He was always smiling and the center of attention. Later I discovered he was a LaVey fan and a de facto Satanist.

I'd often see him chatting up the office hotties, most of them jockeying for his attention. He had no real power within the organization, he was not immensely talented, and he was just about broke. But his office was next to mine and one day as I ate lunch at my desk, the moaning I heard coming from beyond the wall confirmed my suspicions that he had something special. "What was going on in there," I asked after his guest departed. He smiled and said, "Oh that was just Gabriel eating out my ass."

With that in mind, knowing that creating the Warlock Self means *the whole package* (not any specific part) is what gets you across the finish line.

The use of total image put forth in *The Satanic Witch* holds true for the Warlock as well, but with a significant difference; the Warlock can't just *play* the part; he must be the part! The outside appearance and swagger will only be effective if the true Self has been developed to the degree that the Warlock believes he is what he is presenting to the world. Walking the walk creates the confidence essential to excellence and attractiveness. Smart women will know in seconds if the confidence is real or bullshit. As above, so below!

Lazy (and un-Satanic) Warlocks dismiss changing into a more desirable Archetype, claiming that makes them poseurs or phonies. Only a fool thinks Lesser Magic is a switch that flips the moment you throw on a black shirt or a pair of pointy boots. If your true Self is a slob, your inner Warlock innately knows it, and will broadcast that slob to the outside world no matter how many Baphomet medallions you wear. You are who you believe you are, but transformation requires effort! If you think that perfect 10" Witch you covet is going to throw herself onto your couch while you scarf pizza and beer, you're in for a rude awakening. Your mind knows you're a schlub, and so does the rest of the world, so get to work!

USING GREATER AND LESSER MAGIC

By fine tuning lycanthropic abilities through Lesser and Greater Magic, along with using the **Five Points of Pentagonal Power** – a system that can literally transform him into the Satanic (Were)wolf – the Warlock can alter and improve his entire being.

This ability is sometimes innate, but it can also be created, developed, exercised, and applied like any other mental tool. It happens with practice, practice, and more practice. Personality is malleable: It is not cast in stone as once believed. Author Malcom Gladwell wrote in his bestselling book *Outliers* that it takes roughly 10,000 hours of practice to become expert in any discipline. His theory may be up for debate (considering the natural talents of prodigies and fast learners) but the basic premise holds true that practice of any kind will eventually make perfect.

The Satanic Warlock, by embracing the Satanic worldview of himself as his own personal god, enters the playing field with a psychological advantage. He creates his own world by mastering his words and actions. This knowledge, when applied using Greater and Lesser magic, can have a profound effect on weaker personality traits.

"Do not accept the roles that society foists on you. Recreate yourself by forging a new identity, one that commands attention and never bores the audience. Be the master of your own image rather than letting others define it for you. Incorporate dramatic devices into your public gestures and actions – your power will be enhanced and your character will seem larger than life."
–Robert Greene, *The 48 Laws of Power.*

This is the Warlock's "jumping off point," but transformation doesn't happen overnight. The process is fully dependent on which raw materials the Warlock brings to the table. A nerd hoping to transform into a Gentleman will need more time than someone already equipped with the right looks, build and natural swagger. Constant practice, mindfulness, and, above all, belief in himself and the Satanic principle that rewards action will prevail. As the old saw says, "There's no growth in a comfort zone, and no comfort in a growth zone."

IDENTIFY THE ARCHETYPE – THE MAGIC OF MIND

Study Chapter 2 until you identify the Warlock Archetype or composite Archetype you feel best conveys your true Self, so you can begin the process and ritual of mentally and physically changing via the techniques and tools to follow.

Once his Archetype is chosen, the Warlock begins by keeping the mental picture of his ideal Self in his mind for several days, constantly picturing himself as that new Self, reinforcing the image through actions and playing out favorable scenarios of conquest and success. This simple exercise builds new pathways in the brain, seeding the mind with the desired new information. Science has learned that the brain is actually capable of making new connections (called neuroplasticity) that ultimately change a person's very being. Your constant reinforcement facilitates the building of those new pathways.

What's more, positive and pleasurable old memories blurred by the conscious mind may still affect and motivate your current actions. That hot sexual encounter from age 18 may seem distant when you're 40, but it is embedded in your mind's pleasure centers, and will create a stronger feeling of euphoria and confidence than any fabricated scenario you see in a magazine or video.

Continuing to visualize the "mind movie" of the new Self works to integrate the new information into the Warlock's brain, reinforcing his newfound reality. What the Warlock genuinely believes he is ultimately becomes what he really is!

The new mind movie must also replace any and all negative images – physical or mental – through the process of visualization. Replay the bad memories, re-written with new and positive outcomes. The old Warlock self-image must literally be replaced with the new Self.

This powerful repetition in the mind, coupled with the Satanic male ego's need for satisfaction and growth yields powerful results. The Warlock is preparing the unconscious mind to ultimately work on autopilot. After enough time and repetition, along with a healthy dose of magic and adherence to the Five Points of Pentagonal Power, the Warlock Self emerges quite naturally.

This exercise echoes a modern acting technique called "performance from the inside out." In this method, an actor uses vocal and physical expressions that emanate from inner impulses to create an on-stage character. He believes he is the character. The Warlock uses this technique to connect with his inner purpose – the Archetype – employing his lifetime of positive psychological and sociological experiences to get into the part.

When the Warlock is "on," he enters what psychologists call the flow state, where no conscious control is exerted over the act being performed. It's like riding a bike, which becomes automatic once the skill is learned. During development, the new Self virtually suspends reality – a task that is not as uncommon as it sounds. Consider what happens when you're engrossed in a film or TV show: You lose track of the *you* sitting and watching and replace it with a you in the world you're seeing. You're actually just watching images on a screen – but reality, as far as your mind is concerned, is the projection. Your mind *believes* the story is really happening and that you're a part of it. You enjoy being tricked into living in the new world. And in many cases (masturbation for one) the experience is a sensual delight. This will also happen when you've mastered your new Self – you will *become* that Warlock!

THE UNCONSCIOUS IS IN CONTROL

We believe we have free will, but it's not that simple. Numerous psychological studies conclude that our conscious mind is almost totally directed by our *unconscious* mind. This is the stuff of real magic. This unconscious network of billions of connections, experiences, behaviors, and training creates who we are and how the world perceives us.

So when the Warlock makes the new Self a part of his unconscious, it eventually takes over and *that* Self becomes the reality. All those around him see only the new Warlock, the manifestation of his chosen and practiced Archetype.

The more the Warlock practices being his Archetype, uses ritual magic, and applies the Five Points of Pentagonal Power, the stronger the new Self becomes. The more he wears the clothes and acts the part, the more he sees he is that person. His "is-to-be" is complete.

"Knowing is not enough, we must apply. Willing is not enough, we must do."
– Johann Wolfgang von Goethe

A NOTE ON USING LESSER AND GREATER MAGIC – HARNESSING THE FORCES OF DARKNESS

Church of Satan canon provides a rich resource on the practice of Lesser and Greater Magic, so we won't reiterate. Warlocks can always refresh their memories by rereading the books or searching the Church of Satan website. What we will say is that "walking the walk" of your Archetype and using the dark forces of Lesser and Greater ritual magic will reinforce your desired results and speed your transformation. You have the magic at hand – use it!

PENTAGONAL POWER – STEPS IN CREATING THE WARLOCK SELF

The Warlock must master the **Five Points of Pentagonal Power** in order to create his ideal Self. The visual representation of the exercise includes three lower points: **Mind, Physical**, and **Speech**. When combined, they create a powerful combination of **Confidence** and **Charisma**. The ultimate result, the exemplary Warlock Self, holds the key to success on every plane.

Developing each area takes a mixture of plain old common sense and diligent training. The goal is to manifest the ideal, exemplary Warlock; attractive, charismatic and confident. Not every Warlock craves the spotlight: some are quite content to operate in the shadows and may at first employ only some of the five points. But the principles should be understood and practiced, then kept in the "back pocket" because you never know when you'll be called upon to stand and deliver!

THE FIVE POINTS OF PENTAGONAL POWER

MIND

As noted, preparing the mind requires the Warlock to employ visualization, repetition, and positive reinforcement of the chosen Archetype in order to create a lycanthropic transformation into his ideal Warlock *Self*. This is ground zero for everything to come. Once the mind is sufficiently prepared and trained, the other points of power will fall into place, meaning you must practice the exercises and mental methods as often as possible. Don't be impatient. Using these methods in tandem with Lesser and Greater Magic will yield results.

Every Warlock will progress at his own pace, depending on his level of practice and commitment. As is true in all Satanism, results flow only from intention and follow-through. The Warlock must do in order to reap his rewards.

"I learned that willpower, the intensity of desire, and practice can take us to levels of performance we never thought possible.

When we focus deeply on whatever is before us, we slowly gain greater powers of mental perception and we are able to see deeper and deeper into things. We see the connections between phenomena. We awaken higher levels of intelligence. We are hardly aware of the powers we actually possess when we focus this lens," writes Robert Greene, author of The 48 Laws of Power, The Art of Seduction, both de facto

Satanic books.

Steps to conditioning the Mind:

• Establish the Archetype in the mind – focus the will to accept the transformation

• Study and absorb all possible actions, images, and desires of the Archetype

• Constantly visualize specific manifestations of success while *being* the Archetype

• Play the Archetype mind movies regularly, featuring the Warlock as the star

• Replace all negative feelings with the new Archetype image

• Repeat constantly that the new Archetype is the "is-to-be"

PHYSICAL

The simplest and most obvious area of change is in the Warlock's appearance (as discussed in Chapter 2). Although we can learn a great deal about the male physique from its position on the the the LaVey Personality Synthesizer Clock, we must also understand that profound physical change *can* happen in order to facilitate a newly desired Self!

Lycanthropic transformation is a first cousin to shape shifting. Folklore suggests that merely putting on a wolfskin cloak or belt will change the way one walks, looks, and even smells! As LaVey wrote in his essay on *How to Become a Werewolf*, the mere sensation of being an animal will cause certain parts of the body to respond in kind. This is the basis for the physical changes during the Satanic Warlock's (Were)wolf transmogrification.

Once the Archetype is chosen, the Warlock at first just mimics that style (i.e., hair, clothes, body language) to initiate the transformation process. This may sound simple, but it's not as easy as it looks. A bald Warlock for example, needs to make a choice. If he wants his look to include hair, he needs to buy a wig or invest in surgical hair replacement. The Satanic approach is of course to *embrace and exploit* the characteristics you can't change. Not all Black Metal warlocks have waist-length locks! Tell Rob Halford or Joe Satriani they'll never make it without hair.

A short, fat Warlock might not seem like the obvious choice as the Romantic Rake, but what kind of Warlock would you be if you're not up to a challenge? Change what you can and change how you *present* what you can't. You're not getting any taller (boots might add an inch or two), but you certainly *could* lose some weight (if you were willing to go that route).

But why not forget looks entirely and publish a book of your love poetry or learn to play the lute?

Warlocks who do want radical physical changes may take this opportunity to get serious about diet and exercise, transforming their bodies to suit their new Archetype. The good news is they will be rewarded either way. A less than perfect body will be overlooked if the whole "package" sends the right message. As LaVey said in *The Satanic Bible*, "Good looks are unnecessary, but 'looks' certainly are needed."

Of course, use common sense when it comes to clothing. Portly Warlocks should avoid tight T-shirts or horizontal stripes, and skinny Warlocks (unless going for a rocker look) should cover up their puny arms. Choose clothing that fits your Archetype and flatters your strong suits while camouflaging the rest. A word of advice: Solicit the help of a trusted Witch. Women are far more attuned to these matters and can usually tell a man what looks best and works for his chosen image.

Once everything is acquired, the Warlock's next step is to put on the clothes, array his hair, add his chosen accessories, and view (admire!) himself in the mirror as much as possible. This may feel silly at first, but the transmission of visual information – so crucial to the male of the species – is essential to cement the persona in the Warlock's mind. The clothes should be worn at home and in public. This isn't a Halloween costume: It's a permanent transformation. The Warlock must be that Archetype while interacting with people and performing his everyday tasks. The clothes must also be worn in Greater Magic rituals, further melding the Archetype.

It is absolutely essential you "live the part" of your chosen type. Go beyond what's listed here. Find men who embody your chosen Archetype, study their clothing and accessories, hairstyles (including facial hair if applicable), and gather the elements of your look. This is applied costuming (not make-believe cosplay) at its best. Once attired, the Warlock takes on the persona. The more the Warlock "lives" in these clothes, the more and faster he will transform. As noted in Chapter 2, the Warlock must study his iconic Archetypes until everything about them becomes second nature. Really walk in their shoes.

Australian actor F. Matthias Alexander created the Alexander Technique of acting, which is used to recognize and overcome reactive, habitual limitations in movement and thinking. He said, "People do not decide their futures, they decide their habits, and thus habits decide their futures."

This sounds like a joke but isn't: Two guys (myself and some other schlub) walk into job interview for a New York ad agency. Guy #1 (me) is dressed as a pizza delivery guy, replete with pizza box in hand, and Guy #2 is in a cheap Sears suit. The interviewer looked shocked, asked who ordered the pizza, and wants to know where's the other candidate? I stood up and said, "I'm the other candidate." "You," she asked. "Yes," I answered. "You want someone creative. Well, who do you think sent you that resume in the pizza box last week?" I got the job. True story.

PHYSICAL/Body Language

Posture also plays an important part in how the Warlock is perceived. "Walk tall" is great advice, particularly for the Warlock who needs to be seen as edgy, dominant, and even a bit evil. Men who walk with their heads down and shoulders hunched look like pathetic beaten scroungers. Every Warlock must walk with head erect and back straight, no matter his Archetype.

When sitting, don't slump and never cross your legs like a woman. If you want to appear relaxed, lean your dominant arm against a solid object, cock your head to the side as if you're waiting for someone, and use your free hand to hold an object (glass, cigar or cigarette, book, eyeglasses).

When approaching or meeting someone for the first time, gender must be considered. When meeting another man, stand squared to his body with head erect and make eye contact. Extend the handshake and grip firmly (no "flabby fish" handshakes). Allow him to move back or exit to another part of the area first. Stand your ground unless you need to move away quickly.

Men are easy. Negotiating space with a woman is different. Never approach her straight on, as she will find it too aggressive. Move in from an angle to create the feeling she's "allowing" you into her space. Once there, position your body to align with her genital area. Lock eyes and take her wrist gently in your left hand while you shake her hand with your right. Hold it tightly but gently and pull her ever so slightly (almost imperceptibly) toward you.

Smile when you greet both men and women, regardless of mood or expectations about your character. A smile has intense diabolical power.

PHYSICAL/Exercise

We all know about aerobic exercise. Besides the obvious benefit of a stronger, fitter, and more sexually attractive body, workouts open the gates to the mind. The Warlock need not be in top physical condition, but a regular and consistent rigorous workout gets the heart pumping and allows the Warlock to break a sweat, bringing him closer to his goal. Aerobic exercise also works as a form of meditation (running, walking, hiking, strenuous yoga, martial arts, playing a sport, or other physical movement that pushes respiration). Once the body is occupied, the inner (unconscious/subconscious) mind is freed and is ripe for suggestion and visualization. Once again, the "zone" opens up and the Warlock can solidify his Archetype in his mind's eye.

Still not convinced? Regular exercise has been found to spark the "brain-derived neurotropic factor" (BDNF) that actually feeds the brain, which in turn creates neuron growth. Science has discovered that BDNF helps learning, memory, and deeper thinking and can be accomplished with as little as 20 minutes of aerobic exercise. This boost is a direct benefit to Warlocks looking to seed their minds with new Archetypes.

A regular exercise routine will also build stamina and plateau levels that will provide for a second wind in times of need (sexual performance!). This may take many months to accomplish, but the physical and mental benefits can be astounding.

PHYSICAL/Scent

NEVER underestimate the power of your scent. The role and allure of animal smell is discussed more in depth in the chapter on Seduction, but suffice it to say that a distinct masculine odor is an integral part of the Warlock's overall Charisma. A hint of underarm perspiration, other "male" scents like tobacco, sandalwood, and leather along with colognes and soaps consciously and unconsciously transmit signals to everyone around you. Too sweaty and you're considered gross: too sweet and flowery and you're considered effeminate. Balance is struck through trial and error. Experiment and gauge the reaction from both females and males, then choose your most appealing and memorable scent.

SPEECH

It may not be obvious, but a man's speech is a crucial element of his personality (and a key component of the Five Points of Pentagonal Power). Don't underestimate this part of your persona. Speaking too fast, too slow, mumbling, and odd (but often interesting) accents all contribute to how you are perceived, how you're judged, and how people gauge your intelligence. We've all experienced situations when we can't understand what people are saying because they talk too fast, mumble, or their accents are too thick.

Many great actors are instantly recognizable by voice alone. Sounds, like smells, create deep impressions and responses.

Satanists are well aware that a forcefully spoken word in Ritual calls in lust and emotional excitement. Speaking the Infernal names sparks great power. The same is true with common language. Words matter. Flatter someone, and his or her mind and body respond miraculously, recalling the compliment throughout the day and assigning positive feelings to their memory of you, building your appeal. Debase someone and they cower and shrink into their insecurities – or just get mad.

The power of words lies not only in their meaning, but also in the way they are delivered. Don't be in a hurry. Slow down and speak deliberately, adding pauses for people to absorb what you say. A pause also gives the other person a chance to speak, and makes them aware that you are listening to them. Listening, as you'll learn in the chapter on Seduction, is a powerful aphrodisiac. Consider some of the language in *The Satanic Bible*, and how it creates powerful visual and emotional stimuli: *Partake of the elixir of ecstasy … in whose hands the sun is a glittering sword and the moon is a through-thrusting fire … Open the mysteries of your creation.* All these conjure clear and forceful images, giving the speaker a real air of power!

The Warlock must understand the complexity and sophistication of this tool, he must make effective speech a foundation of his overall magical workings.

So how does it all work? The key components of effective speech include breath, phonation (how breath creates sound), resonation (amplification of the sound), and articulation. Using speech correctly will change any voice into an instrument of persuasion.

The breath starts in the belly (diaphragm) not the lungs, and is produced when a combination of several body parts work in tandem. Recognizing that your speech will be affected by how you breathe is essential to the proper mastery of speech. Feel your breath by placing your hand on your diaphragm as you speak. Take deep belly breaths with every sound you are trying to make. Work deep, not hard. Digging deep and projecting your words with the belly breath supporting you will give your voice a much more commanding tone (phonation), vibrating the vocal chords to create a richer sound.

Resonation (amplification) of the sound also uses the breath as it travels through your upper body and head. Your conscious effort to use the breath can make the articulation of speech weak or strong, depending on its depth. Concentrating on accessing the deep breath before each impulse to speak will create a superior (and quite seductive) effect.

To properly articulate words, the Warlock must be aware of his tongue, lips, and the rest of his mouth. Most people are lazy with articulation. They mumble or slur, creating an impression of stupidity or laziness. Notice how your words are formed in all the parts of the mouth. Roll the vowels around and feel which part controls which sound. Use your tongue and facial muscles. Be deliberate and clear when pronouncing each word and your message will never be misunderstood!

THE ULTIMATE GOAL – Confidence and Charisma

Developing, strengthening, and most importantly *regularly practicing* each of the lower three Points of Power (Mind, Physical and Speech), brings these forces together to create the ultimate goal – Confidence and Charisma. These two qualities combine to complete and project the desired Archetype, elevating the Warlock to godlike status.

CHARISMA – The Invisible Aphrodisiac and How to Get It

Everyone knows it when they see it. We all know people who have it, and we have all fallen victim to it in spite of all efforts to resist. But few can really define the extremely powerful quality known as *charisma* or *charm*.

The word "charm" is rooted in the Latin *carmen* (a song or incantation tied to a spell). Witches use Charisma to create "*glamour*," from the Scottish gramarye (magic, enchantment, spell). They use this technique on their prey, employing their arsenal of wiles, beauty, whispers, and hypnotic gazes. The result is an invisible yet palpable essence, the innate aphrodisiac that clouds people's minds and makes the spell caster irresistible despite any physical or social shortcomings.

Unlike the Witch whose beauty can (and will) transfix a man forever if necessary, the Warlock's good looks may get a woman's attention, but if he doesn't immediately reinforce that positive response with Charisma, she will leave him for a man who will.

Let's break Charisma down into three simple techniques:

1) **Eye contact and Immersion in the Subject.** During your conversation, pay close, unflinching attention to your partner. Listen intently and ask probing questions. Make that person believe he or she is the most fascinating person in the world. Use the "boomerang" technique – repeating key words the person says to prove you're listening. And DON'T shift the conversation back to the subject of you!

2) **Inject humor.** Never be dead serious unless the conversation warrants. Match the mood, but smile and laugh whenever possible.

3) **Touch the person.** Use touch in a gentle, non-threatening, and non-creepy manner. Shake a man's hand firmly (no vise grip), but gently grasp a woman's hand in your two hands. Casually touch a forearm when making a point.

Following these rules in every personal encounter will build your Charisma until it becomes second nature.

On a personal note, I have often observed Playboy's Hugh Hefner, paying special attention to how he acted in group situations. Not surprisingly, Hefner always focused on the women in the group, making eye contact, asking questions, and making sure they were taken care of. He ignored all the men unless asked a specific question. Hefner adores women and it shows. Women describe him as having abundant Charisma – undoubtedly the reason he's attracted so many young women throughout his life (and is again married to a much younger woman) – he's 90 years old!

So no excuses, Warlocks. Get to work on your Charisma… *before* you're 90!

CONFIDENCE - The Warlock's Calling Card

Charisma is just one of the two top Points of Power. The other Point is Confidence.

Of all of the qualities that combine to express the ideal Warlock Self, Confidence is the most important. Without Confidence, Charisma struggles to surface. Without Confidence, even extreme physical attractiveness is all but useless. Confidence is the Warlock's calling card. It sets him apart from the self-loathing and self-conscious herd. It gives him the ability to master a subject or confront a foe without fear of failure (more on the problem of fear in Chapter 5).

Like Charisma, Confidence is tricky to define. Confidence is an amorphous quality that broadcasts a Warlock's belief in himself no matter what the circumstance. It allows him not to buckle under physical or mental pain.

Confidence doesn't cower in the face of competition and it doesn't abandon the Warlock after losses or setbacks. Confidence pushes on in the face of adversity and increases regardless of victories or defeats. Simply put, it is true belief that a man can handle whatever is thrown at him.

Of course the Warlock must not confuse Confidence with stupid risk-taking or acts of false bravado executed simply to impress. Confidence is not arrogance; it doesn't appear and disappear. *It is a constant* in the true Warlock Self – as much a part of him as the way he walks or the tone of his voice. Confidence is part and parcel of personality. And above all, it cannot be faked. It is a palpable aura that other human beings recognize, and in most cases respond to favorably.

The Witches interviewed for this book confirm that Confidence is the single most appealing and attractive quality a man can possess.

—A good personality [confidence] makes you more attractive. I'm much more attracted to people based on their intelligence and manners rather than their physical being.

—Personality and confidence. Looks and dress are eye-catching and may open doors (and legs), but without the personality and confidence to go to the next level, good looks and swagger aren't going to lead to anything meaningful.
    —I want someone whose physical presence comes in as loud and clear (and of course appealing) as his intellectual presence. I'm recalling that old E.F. Hutton commercial: When this man enters a room, the collective intake of breath could take down the wallpaper. Height, style, good looks, and an air of total confidence without arrogance.

—Women are looking for power — not necessarily muscles, but a confidence and commanding presence that communicates strength and surety, and the promise of security for her and for her offspring.

So the obvious question is: How does a Warlock gain maximum Confidence? Simply stated, like Charisma, it is the end product generated from the lower Points of Power. Confidence can be also broken into its components of intention, decisiveness, and follow-through.

Treat every situation as an opportunity for you to project your "is-to-be" into the world. Keep your memories of achievements, sexual conquests, and other milestone successes in the foreground of your consciousness, and you will naturally exude Confidence. If you believe in yourself wholeheartedly, others will too.

The most important secret to building and exuding Confidence is, that the more the Warlock *faces and overcomes* challenges, fears, failures, adversity, criticism, and heartbreak, the more Confidence he has.

A male porn star (let's call him Tom) who became a good friend of mine was the victim of the "Irish curse," better known as a small penis. To make matters worse, although the average man is about five inches, in Tom's line of work anything under seven inches is considered small. Whenever he whipped it out at a shoot, directors groaned, knowing they had to do extra work angling the cameras to make him look larger. But what he lacked in size he made up for in enthusiasm, which was all the girls cared about. His mystery and passion showed through whenever he was making love to a woman — on or off camera (as many of his girls would attest). Tom is one of the most sought after actors in the business. He makes every girl cum. You should too.

"There's one blessing only, the source and cornerstone of beatitude — confidence in self." — Roman philosopher Seneca (tutor to Nero)

KEYS TO CONFIDENCE

1) No matter what the circumstance, situation, relationship, or project, address it with steadfast purpose! Know your desired outcome go-

ing in, and enter the arena with only your goal in mind. Walk, talk, and use your body to project an air of defined purpose. You must communicate that you know what you want. Don't ask for opinions if you don't want them. It is better to ask forgiveness than permission.

2) Once you set your purpose, make the decision! Don't flip flop! Make up your mind! This is a major part of Confidence. Decisiveness reads as an unwavering faith in yourself and your ideas. It's sexy.

3) Don't be a paper tiger. Nobody respects a phony or a quitter. See your tasks through regardless of the pitfalls, setbacks, pain, or potential failure. This increases your personal power with you and your peers, and adds to your overall Confidence.

"As soon as you trust yourself, you will know how to live." – Johann Wolfgang von Goethe.

warlock wisdom

- Identify and be your chosen Satanic Archetype in mind and body.

- You are who you believe you are – transform into your true (Were)Wolf.

- Practice, practice, practice becoming the exemplary Archetype – live the persona.

- Good looks help, but are not crucial in creating a new Self.

- Be brutally honest about how you're perceived – just "being yourself" may be holding you back.

- An effective image trumps physical shortcomings.

- Use the power of Mind to constantly create the new Self.

- The three foundation Points of Pentagonal Power combine to create Charisma and Confidence.

- Confidence is the single most important aspect of the exemplary Warlock.

THE SATANIC GENTLEMAN –
"A MAN OF WEALTH AND TASTE"

"Neither a boor, nor an oaf be."

Society expects Warlocks to be (and look) "evil," black-clad and adorned with occultnik symbols, pentagrams, or Baphomets the size of dinner plates around their necks. Walk into any room, the rubes think, and the air turns cold, and the ladies' panties get wet.

After all, Satan himself has always been a trickster. Playing that card can be fun if the occasion calls for legitimate adornments or the mood strikes. The spooky look will always shake up civilians. Antiheroes are indeed sexy, and when combined with the "S-word," the combination can be downright intoxicating. But what the Warlock must keep in mind is that whether he flaunts the macabre or adopts another Archetype, his "style" and gentlemanly stature matter. This potent mixture of Sex and Wonder meld together to create his outward appearance and often allow him to overcome a number of natural physical and social short-comings.

Many a regular guy who works his ass off in a 9-to-5 job and embraces his Warlock Self after hours finds great success in social gatherings and seductions by letting his unique style shine through. Like the old song says, "The minute you walked in the joint, I could see you were a man of distinction." And that's the Warlock's goal: to be immediately viewed as an "above the crowd" sophisticate, ready for anything the world can throw at him. But your actions have to back it up. People will remember your actions.

Throughout my travels I have met many men who, when judged on the surface alone can be easily criticized for some obvious shortcomings: "He's five foot three. He has huge ears. He has a beer gut and hobbit feet. He chews with his mouth open. He's as skinny as a bean pole (and about as alluring). He puts ice in his white zinfandel. He has no idea how to dress." These are all less-than-stellar traits, BUT... many of these can be overcome with a little education, exercise, and *personality.*

Jackie Gleason was a fat man. He had a closet full of expensive suits in various sizes to accommodate his fluctuating girth. Gleason never tried to pretend he wasn't fat; instead he used the "disadvantage" to create *The Great One*, his memorable, larger-than-life persona. He was an impeccable gentleman, always in a suit that fit him perfectly. He never squeezed into anything tight or wore anything that was too big for him.

Many a young lady has confided in me that she's more concerned with the fit and quality of a man's clothes than she is with his physique. I've been told a number of times that I have a "white man's flat ass," but I make sure my pants fit well, especially in the seat. Mission accomplished, as long as she doesn't see the truth until after my pants come off!

WHAT IS STYLE?

Style is Lesser Magic manifested as "knowing what to do and how to act." Style is an immediate declaration of attitude and stature that encompasses all social circumstances. Style intimates likes and interests, social ability, financial status, and individuality – all cornerstones of Confidence. Warlocks never enter anyone's lair uninvited, nor do they disrespect or brutalize anyone's possessions. Style is grace and flair and the command to look. When a Warlock is successful with his personal style, the Italians call it *sprezzatura* (the art of making the difficult look effortless). Style sets the Warlock apart from the "great unwashed."

Although it's nearly impossible to catalog all the elements of personal style, what follows are some generally accepted key guidelines for gentlemen, regardless of social strata. It doesn't matter if the Warlock is the Black Metal Rocker or the Everyman; all Warlocks must know the building blocks of style.

WARDROBE

Warlocks should never be slaves to fashion fads, as our identities hinge on individualism. But your clothing and accessories speak volumes and. when chosen correctly, they immediately express your Archetype. Your "look" telegraphs the physical shape of your body, your financial status, and your overall degree of sex appeal. The style of clothing a Warlock chooses of course depends on his Archetype. He may employ many different styles, layers, and accessories, but what is of paramount importance is quality and fit. Cheap clothes can be spotted a mile away – especially by women. Cheap suit jokes abound, and for good reason. It is far better to invest in one or two high quality items than a dozen pieces of crap. They'll last much longer and always look good if you take care of them. If you're naturally not a clotheshorse and pay little attention to clothing, ask a woman's advice; they're often experts on fabric, fit, and style.

Fit is absolutely essential. Bespoke clothing (made to measure, with your own choices of fabric and cut) is of course ideal, but prohibitively expensive to most of the population. But you don't have to have your clothing custom made to have it properly tailored. A skilled tailor costs less than you think, and will dramatically improve even a lesser-quality suit.

Regardless of the style, pants and shirts should never be too big or too small. Squeezing 10 pounds of shit into a five-pound bag just says you are completely out of touch with how you look, as does swimming in an over-sized parachute of a shirt. Nothing says hand-me-downs like a too-long shirtsleeve or a collar that can fit another head. NEVER succumb to any passing fad that you know is ridiculous (no matter how cute the salesgirl is).

Suit (or sports) jackets and coats should never be too long or too short. It may sound strange, but many men don't have a clue about their options. If you're short, choose a short jacket or coat, marked with an "S," like 40S. If you're fat and/or tall, go to the big men's shop and be fitted properly. Your body is an instrument and should be adorned appropriately.

Overcoats should be large enough to fit over a suit jacket or heavy sweater.

Jackets should lie flat across your back and shoulders, with no space where the collar meets your neck. Sleeves should be just short enough to show some shirtsleeve. Casual jackets should close with some breathing room around the waist but fit snugly on the chest.

Pants vary depending on style, and many are a matter of personal taste. Whatever you choose should fit your Archetype. The Rocker may live in jeans (from skinny to ragged) and the Gentleman may only wear dress trousers. Each has its own rule from tight fit to comfortable. Dress pants should always fit with just about an inch of room in the waist, not too baggy in the rear (all women evaluate men's asses) and cuffs should break just above the shoe – no high waters.

And if you're brave enough, many women find kilts impossible to resist!

Choose your formalwear color based on the time of day and type of function. Tails are usually worn for "white tie" events. "Formal" means tuxedos or dinner jackets. Black is appropriate any time, while white is usually only worn in the daytime, and during spring and summer.

Bow ties should be of the "tying" variety rather than clip-on. This gives the Warlock an immediate edge of sophistication, and they're not that difficult to tie. (The Internet has dozens of instructional videos.)

Short pants in most cases should be avoided unless you're auditioning for a "Little Rascals" revival or live on the Equator.

Shirts and sweaters must also fit your Warlock Archetype and are particularly central to masculinity as they immediately differentiate the sexes. Suffice it to say, sleeves should never be too long, sweaters and shirts never too tight (unless you are deliberately muscular and flaunt it), and T-shirts should flatter the body (tight if you're built, looser if you're not).

Shoes are also a matter of personal taste, but women NOTICE men's shoes and they say a lot about the wearer. The "cheap" rule applies here as well: Cheap shoes will fall apart quickly and make you look like a bum. Good leather shoes and boots, when properly cared for, will outlast 10 pairs of cheap shoes and boots and always make you look devil-ishly swank. Polish and brush them after each wearing. If your shoes get wet DON'T dry them with a blow dryer or on a heating vent. Let them dry naturally and polish or brush them when they're dry to bring them back to life.

Hats can be wonderful adornments and add swagger to your style. Please remember to remove hats when indoors (unless you're attending a costume party), and it never hurts to tip them when a lady's present.

PEACOCKING

Warlocks create their own unique look and swagger, often inspired by an affinity for a particular time period or style. These "looks" not only push the boundaries of their Archetypes; some also stray beyond what's typically defined as masculine, especially when it comes to artists and musicians. Many outfits are androgynous or even effeminate. Using these sartorial tools can be a powerful way of "peacocking," or display-ing flair well beyond the ordinary, which many women find irresistible.

But the caveats of proper dress still apply, even to the more Bohemian looks. Fit is essential, colors have to work with skin tones, and the entire look needs to express the Warlock's Archetype without compromising his message of masculinity. This requires thoughtful combinations and an eye for balance. Flowing silk pirate shirts and heavy leather boots create a sexy swashbuckling image for the Rocker or Rake, but an eye patch (most of the time) goes too far. Makeup and hats can make the Romantic both foppish and roguish, and capes can add a dramatic dash to the Creative. Be careful not to tip the balance too far in any one direc-tion unless you're deliberately attempting to unleash your feminine side.

Musicians are great at peacocking. Many not-so-great musicians get over just because "they're in a band" or look like a pirate about to steal some booty (the fleshy kind). A musician Warlock confided in me that his image is 90 percent of his appeal. He says no one (especially the women) listens that intently to his music; it's the big show that gets their juices flowing.

One night in my youth, I tried the androgynous look. I showed up at

CBGB's in Manhattan in full safety pin punk splendor, including eye makeup applied by a good gal friend, the tightest black jeans I could find, and a made-up band name – I think it was the "Bowery Bums." The night was a bust because, although I had a lot of opportunities (male and female) thrown my way, I got too drunk to take advantage!

GROOMING

Regardless of financial status, career success, or relationship savvy, there's no easier way to express security and confidence than being properly groomed. Grooming reinforces your standing above the herd and shows self-respect. *Nobody* wants you if you stink!

The level of men's ignorance on the subject of simple hygiene (and how it impacts their interactions) can be astonishing. Warlocks don't need to be "metrosexual," foppish, or vain, but they should certainly learn the basic keys to lasting appeal.

Bathe regularly, especially after physical stress, paying particular attention to areas below the waist. Deodorant can be applied or not, varying from Warlock to Warlock. Mild natural male underarm and pubic scents can be acceptable and play a role as an aphrodisiac (as noted in the chapter on Seduction). But overpowering underarm or genital odor should be avoided. Scrub the penis, anus and testicle areas well (be considerate of the lady who might have her nose there). Scent is a powerful aphrodisiac, but odor is not.

Colognes and aftershaves can be a positive accessory to overall grooming *if not too heavy.* Use sparingly! This is a good rule of thumb: if you use a fragrance, someone should have to be touching you to smell it.

Hair, no matter what length or style, should always be cut and styled well (and clean!). Spring for a real barber instead of the national chain barbershops unless you sport a buzz cut.

Hair dye can be a dramatic way to bring out certain Archetypes as well as covering gray. Unless you're trying to look like Wayne Newton, *please* have it professionally done. The aging Warlock should be mindful about coming off as "trying too hard" when covering gray hair. Beware of too-dark grocery store dyes that make your head look like a Q-tip dipped in shoe polish.

Beards and mustaches should be trimmed regularly unless your Archetype calls for a radical or even scruffy look. Still, nothing is as disturbing as a mustache or beard full of leftover lunch.

Groom nose hair, ear hair, and eyebrows – especially for the older Warlock.

Fingernails and toenails must be clean and trimmed. File any sharp edges.

Brush and floss your teeth, and use mouthwash regularly. Have bad teeth repaired and whitened if needed. Your smile is one of the first things a woman notices. Bad breath is not only offensive but it may also indicate serious health issues. It will stop seduction dead in its tracks!

SOCIAL GRACES – BE THE "ANTI-BOOR"

It can't be overstressed – a Satanic gentleman strives to be the "anti-boor," in both word and deed. Ideally he makes everyone around him feel comfortable (or uncomfortably curious). Employing the social graces sets the scene, adding wonder and an air of mystery to the Warlock's overall diabolical Self.

Conversely, bad manners or ignorance of the social graces can make even an Adonis look like a schlub. Never mind that ignorance and solipsism are thoroughly Un-Satanic. Manners are easy to learn and cost nothing, but the lack thereof can be disastrous. The Warlock must always be aware of his surroundings and respect the feelings (and lairs) of those with whom he interacts. Regardless of a Warlock's station in life, if he conducts himself in a civilized and polished manner he will be seen as the sophisticated Devil that he is. You know what they say about the Devil's manners!

Not many people (including employees of Playboy Enterprises) ever see the inside of the Playboy Mansion. Most gatherings are held outdoors near the Grotto and zoo. But I did see the inner sanctum numerous times, by virtue of showing manners and respect not only to my superiors, but to the security personnel that guarded Hefner and his estate, the support personnel, and even the Mansion cook (whom

I'd met through a mutual friend). I looked and acted the part of a refined gentleman. People notice this stuff (especially the Bunnies – but that's another story). So remember: Manners open doors, both literal and figurative.

Here are a few rules for all Warlocks:

WOMEN ALWAYS COME FIRST – CHIVALRY IS DEVILISHLY ATTRACTIVE

Political correctness be damned! Men must take the lead in social situations. Despite feminist claptrap, most women still love the idea of chivalry, meaning it should be employed by all Warlocks!

Women come first when ordering meals, opening doors, (except entering elevators, in which case men enter first and women exit first), making introductions, and any other circumstance where you are in the company of a woman.

Always greet and introduce a woman first when being introduced to a couple or a group.

Women are seated first at a dinner table (and men should push in their chairs).

Open car doors for women and be sure they are properly and safely seated before you enter the car.

Women should always be picked up and men should always drive.

If there is more than one vehicle, always walk her safely to hers.

Be considerate. Although you should arrange the details of a date, never force a woman to do anything she doesn't want to do.

Always pick up your date on time, even if she makes you wait.

Men should stand whenever a woman leaves or returns to a table. Try this the next time you're with another couple. You will score huge points from your partner if the other gents fail in this area.

Always pay for the date. "Dutch treat" is no such thing – it's just cheap. If you can't afford an expensive restaurant or extravagant date, arrange for something modest yet romantic like a concert in the park or moonlit cemetery stroll. This is even more effective when the events caters to her interests.

On city sidewalks, always walk on the curb side. This charming but obsolete custom originated in the days when sewage was thrown into streets and women needed protection from nasty splashes. This is one of my favorite pieces of advice to implement (and certainly the easiest).

One cold and rainy November day, a midtown NYC bus was barreling down Madison Avenue. A woman was on the sidewalk with me, and I stepped in front of her, taking position on the sidewalk for what I knew would be a righteous soaking. I took the splash all over my overcoat in order to keep the lady dry. No, I'm not making it up. And yes, she made it up to me later – in spades!

RELATIONSHIPS

The morning after a date, follow up with a call or text thanking her and saying you enjoyed yourself. If you don't want to pursue the romance, send a polite but clear message like, "I think we could be great friends."

Never kiss and tell.

After three rejections, move on. Do not under any circumstance stalk a woman or make a pest of yourself. This screams weakness (and is possibly dangerous behavior) and will dash any hopes of ever seeing the lady again.

If a relationship ends badly, never gossip about it with your circle of friends.

RESPECT A PERSON'S LAIR

As was astutely put forth in *The Satanic Bible*, a Warlock must always respect another's lair. Always wait to be invited to do anything in someone else's home, whether it be having a drink, sitting in a chair, or looking at some item of interest. NEVER open closets, drawers, medicine cabinets or refrigerator doors unless instructed to do so.

Never show up empty-handed, especially on your first visit. Bring a small gift or gastronomic treat when invited to dinner. A spirit suffices for a cocktail gathering.

Say please and thank you while being served – both food and drinks. Always compliment the chef. Even if you don't like the food, find some thing positive to say about the meal.

Send a thank-you note the next day after a party of any sort. Hand-written notes or cards show the most class, but any format will do.

Do not smoke in a person's home unless it is clearly permitted. If unsure, ask. If there's any hesitation on the part of your host *do not smoke*. If you do smoke, bring your own ashtray. If you are in the company of other smokers, have extras or offer to share yours.

RESPECT ANOTHER MAN'S RELATIONSHIPS

Never seriously flirt with another man's woman.

Never poach another man's girlfriend, tempting as it may be. If she's flirting with you, show mild interest, but wait until she is done with him to pursue in earnest.

Never poach another man's wife – it can get you killed.

If you find yourself in a love triangle, expect things to get messy and uncomfortable, especially if you're "shitting where you eat."

If you find yourself in an extramarital affair, be discreet above all and know it will likely end badly, despite the fact that "it takes two to tango." This is certainly a disastrous scenario, so weigh the pluses and minuses carefully. There are plenty of free women.

TABLE MANNERS

Complicated table settings may seem intimidating, but they're actually quite easy to navigate. Utensils are arranged in the order you will use them (outside to inside), so you just need to choose the utensil farthest from your plate. In America, cut with the right hand, hold the fork with the left, then switch hands to bring the fork to your mouth. In Europe you may fork food with the left hand into your mouth.

Never begin eating before all entrées have been served. The exception is bread placed on the table with drinks, or hot soup if others have not ordered appetizers.

Soup must be eaten with the proper spoon, spooning outward to the edge of the bowl. Never make slurping sounds or blow it cool.

Napkins should be laid across the lap; never anchored around the neck or tucked into the shirt collar. When leaving the table, place the napkin on your chair seat, not the table.

Never "double dip" when hors d'oeuvres or appetizers are served. Always use a plate and napkin. If you can't handle a drink and plate at the same time, find a table.

The best rule for ordering wine in a fine restaurant is *don't fake it*. If you are an expert, wonderful. If not, excuse yourself from the table, find the sommelier (the wine steward), *tip him* and ask him to recommend a mid-range wine to best compliment your party's anticipated meals. This simple but very effective trick gives you overwhelmingly Devilish sophistication and swagger!

Never talk with your mouth full or chew with your mouth open.

PARTY ETIQUETTE

If you're the host, always greet each guest individually. Shake hands and smile. Women whom you know personally can be kissed on the cheek – not on the lips. If lipstick smudges your cheek, never wipe it in the presence of the woman who deposited it. Wear it as a badge of honor and clean it later when you have privacy.

Do not host BYOB parties.

Provide finger foods at cocktail parties.

Provide basic liquor and mixers for standard parties. Make every effort to have favorite spirits on hand for regular friends and guests.

To end a party, start putting the liquor away – folks will get the hint.

Never pressure non-drinkers into imbibing.

Misbehaving guests should be asked to leave.

Offer inebriated guests a place to rest. Never allow them to drive, no matter how much they insist they are "fine."

ETIQUETTE IN THE DIGITAL AGE

The digital revolution has created several new challenges. The instant gratification available via the Internet, social networking, and multi-capable mobile devices often breeds bad manners. These modern marvels may facilitate some very diabolical pursuits, but they also enable laziness, rudeness, bullying, and even cowardice. Nothing is more un-Satanic than caving in to the pressures of online herding.

Satanists must apply the same courtesies on digital platforms as they do in person – especially Warlocks, who should uphold strength of character and set an example as civilized men.

A few simple rules:

Email is a way of life now. Everyone has time to answer emails in a timely fashion. Don't let people think you're ignoring them by not responding. Let your circle know if you're one of the rare birds who doesn't check email often. They won't believe you, but it might avoid some hurt feelings.

Never "ghost" someone or hide from texts. If you don't want to communicate, say so. Don't let your passive-aggressive non-response "speak" for you. The same holds true for Facebook and other social networking platforms. Un-friend or block as needed, but don't ignore (and don't crab about the person to mutual friends either).

Never be a troll or use social networking as a shield for cowardice, bullying, spreading lies, or shaming. Never say anything online that you wouldn't say to someone's face.

Posing, bitching, moaning, and complaining on social media should be avoided at all costs. If you have a legitimate beef with someone, take it up privately. No one wants to sniff your dirty laundry, and if they do they're probably gossiping about you the same way.

ONLINE DATING

Don't create a fake online persona (you know who you are). If possible, be honest about being a Satanist. Not all Satanists are "out" at work, but keeping this key element of your personality secret from a potential relationship will undoubtedly be a deal breaker if it's discovered later. This sounds obvious, but many men think they can get away with fabricating an identity. They may think a woman will forget what you told her or be so mesmerized by you when you actually meet that she will ignore your lies. She won't. This is blatantly wrong and nearly always disastrous. Women can smell a phony a mile away, so if you don't live up to your online credentials you immediately have two strikes against you.

Should you be admitted to any Satanic social media platforms or groups, do not mistake them for dating resources or use what's shared there to fuel your masturbatory fantasies. There are plenty of porn sites for that.

warlock wisdom

- Acting as a proper gentleman is the Way of the Warlock and will always set you apart because Satan is the consummate gentleman.

- Never be a boor.

- Be mindful that "ladies come first" in all matters.

- Stay true to your personal Archetype and style.

- Dress well: quality trumps quantity.

- Pay strict attention to grooming and hygiene.

- Respect another person's lair at all times.

- Respect a woman's feelings even if you have to end a relationship.

- Respect another man's relationships – don't poach.

- "Please and Thank you" are lost arts – revive them and keep them sacrosanct.

- Hone your table manners.

- It's fine to "peacock," but don't be a clown.

- Exercise proper online etiquette – answer emails and texts, and don't hide behind online avatars like a coward.

CHAPTER FIVE

THE SATANIC LAWS OF POWER –
HOW TO BE A GOD!

"To have and wield power you must seduce and charm. You must be cunning and a chess master. You must also know what evil lurks in the hearts of men."

If there ever were a consummate Devil's game, it would have to be power. Besides money and women, Warlocks want power more than anything else. Admit it. Power is the great equalizer, the means to get women, money, and fame – whatever you want, whenever you want it. It's Satanic in all its magical forms because it grants control over your life and very often the lives of others. Power is the Warlock's yang to the yin wiles of the Satanic Witch. With it, a 6 o'clock man becomes a 12 o'clock Warlock – a god in the eyes of others.

The world has many cultures, and power is universally lusted after across all of them. It is the invisible commodity that separates the haves from the have-nots. Wealth is power, good looks are power, the right connections are power, and they all add up to personal glory and satisfaction. Power is what allows you to do what you want or to not do what you don't want. It's the path to all pleasures.

Many are initially drawn to Satanism by its promise of power. Power over the self, the environment, and others is very seductive and gratifying. Your power makes your enemies irrelevant. Satanism's carnal, life-celebrating philosophy and rebellious aesthetics are a strong and immediately identifiable combination. Warlocks are often perceived as powerful because they are aligned with Satanism.

Much of our current antiseptic, politically correct society unfortunately still clings to the egalitarian nonsense that everyone is the same and should share equally in everything, regardless of their abilities or contributions. Seeking and wielding power for its own sake is not just frowned upon by these nincompoops, but it's also considered opportunistic, egomaniacal, nefarious, and just plain evil. When Satanists hear a list like that they say, "Let's get some!" We don't buy into the fairytale thinking that the world is obligated to shower us with Ferraris and big-screen TVs simply for being born. We're happy to earn our way and equally happy to shun those who refuse to do the same.

This societal mindset, coupled with religious pie-in-the-sky promises designed to keep the masses docile and obedient naturally portrays those seeking power as pariahs. People, especially men who are gun-shy about feminist backlash, not only tiptoe around their lust for power but also cock-block themselves from employing tactics they instinctively know will get them want they want, both professionally and personally.

Fear is the enemy; Satanism is the balm. Warlocks fearful of taking what they want need to trust and embrace their lust for life. An interesting Spanish proverb has God saying, "Take what you want and pay for it." Indeed there are always consequences, but they're worth the effort. It takes balls to take power. Satan has been called many things – but never a eunuch!

In the cave days, the evolving human animal's deep sense of fear was essential, serving to protect him from larger animal attacks and a generally dangerous environment. He lived in an almost constant *fight or flight* mode. That conditioning has followed most of humanity through the centuries, manifesting in the herd as the need for a powerful overseer in the universe – a God or gods – to protect them. The big sky daddy package is also full of guilt and shame to keep the masses in check. It is a high price for the illusion of protection, but an opportunity for those who are naturally beyond the need for such comforting self-delusion.

Being helpless and powerless makes us miserable. In most circumstances, there is always someone who has the upper hand. There are always winners and losers. The Warlock wants to be the winner and does everything in his power to make sure he grabs the brass ring.

Fear and its resulting "moral compass" have to be dealt with in order to have real power over oneself and others. The good news is that (for the most part) power is completely in your control. If you make the right choices (for the right reasons), play the chess game with skill, and use reason instead of allowing your emotional whims to dictate your actions, you will wield great power.

It must be stressed that surrendering to emotion is the primary barrier to power. Ask any Warlock who's compromised himself and fallen for a girl's charms: we don't always think with the right head. Decisions made in the heat of passion seldom turn out well. Be calculating and the keys to your own Hellish kingdom are in your hands. Identify what stands between you and your power and make that your target.

Any man who has tried to be good all of the time is bound to come to ruin among the great number that are not good. Hence a prince who wants to keep his authority must learn how not to be good, and use that knowledge, or refrain from using it, as necessity requires. – Niccolò Machiavelli, *The Prince*

Don't rest on your laurels. Your power must be diligently defended. As most Satanists know, human nature (greed and lust) is always in play, meaning there will always be shit stirrers who think they can steal your power! They will talk about you behind your back, be jealous of you, try to take what's yours, and basically do whatever they can to fuck you over. Don't kid yourself. As much as you think you are invulnerable because someone claims to be your "friend," people will often smile to your face today and talk about you behind your back tomorrow. Much of this talk may be idle chatter or conversation at a party, but they are *talking*. You are a powerful Warlock! You are larger than life, and you're being noticed. Stories about you can be entertaining (and reinforce your Archetype), or they can be downright disastrous gossip. Losers feel like big shots when they trash others because it gives them the illusion of *power* over their own pitiful lives. The old saying, "Keep your friends close and your enemies closer" is a lesson well learned.

ERADICATE FEAR – POWER IS A DIRTY GAME

Seeking and wielding power is not for the faint of heart. What separates Warlocks from the herd when it comes to power is that we subscribe to verse 3:9 of *The Satanic Bible's* Book of Satan. That text demands "an eye for an eye, tooth for tooth, four fold, a hundred fold!" We neutralize the guilt that paralyzes many who seek power because we realize that man, as the ultimate animal, can (and will) turn on us given the chance in order to get what he wants. So why not strike the first blow?

Not long after I was named COO of a major adult video powerhouse based in Barcelona, Spain, one of the salespeople decided her live-in boyfriend should have gotten the position instead of me. Although she smiled at me every day and was polite and cordial, she seethed underneath and conspired to have me fired. Her campaign against me began shortly after I'd produced a tongue-in-cheek video for an industry event that had me sitting in my gothically-styled office, with special effect flames burning around me in typical Satanic fashion.

The bitch, and I use that term purposely, mounted an attack to my superiors, claiming I was a devil worshipper. In short time I was relieved of my duties.

But what the backstabber didn't know was that I had gathered intelligence on her and her maggot boyfriend (as I normally do on all those who work for me – a practice I adopted very early in my career). When I learned she was my enemy, I leaked some damaging information about her and conducted Greater Magic to curse her and her fucktard boyfriend, along with alerting my many high-level friends and colleagues in the business that she was a troublemaker and lazy worker. I also let a very dubious European porn company know that her boyfriend would be a good fit for them. The unfortunate girl somehow suffered a nervous breakdown, lost her job, had difficulties with her mate (who soon failed in his own company affiliated with the porn outfit I set up) and has never been heard from since.

A major part of all fear is the idea of not being liked. We think if people don't like us they won't give us what we want (including themselves) or will shun us, leaving us to live and die alone. The truth is not everyone likes you. Some people even hate you. We're lucky if half the people we interact with really like us at all. This is especially true outside our intimate circle of friends and relatives. Life forces us to deal with people with whom we would never otherwise associate (school, an office full of co-workers, a doctor's office or hospital, the airport). Most humans barely tolerate other humans, and Satanists have very high standards. We are fortunate to have a few genuine friends who truly enjoy our company. Let's be generous and say only 75% of the population actually dislikes us – why not exploit them and their circumstances to get what we want? Once we recognize that our true friends and people we can rely on are a minority, we can then see the world as it really is – ours for the taking – without self-inflicted guilt, doubt or angst.

It's astounding that many believe the great world leaders, the rich and famous, and the captains of industry, all got where they were by being altruistic benefactors. The world's major players know that charity begins at home and serve themselves first. Most have used others as stepping-stones to get ahead, or at the very least had scores of minions to do their dirty work.

By recognizing power as a pragmatic game we see we must rely on ourselves as our only saviors. This liberation strengthens the idea that we can do for ourselves, but more importantly, expands beyond our perceived limits about our fullest potential. Fear stops us from going beyond what's comfortable, killing off growth. We must feel the fear and use it to crash through boundaries, try new things, create, build, and *produce*. When we are forced to fend for ourselves we accomplish what seemed impossible. Think about how you rise to the occasion when faced with a drop-dead deadline. Think about what you've put yourself through physically and mentally to get that big job or win that special someone's heart. You've pressed on against "insurmountable" odds because you wouldn't take no for an answer. Fear served as a goad to success, not a paralyzing obstacle.

Doing something unfamiliar or challenging in the face of fear, then exceeding your expectations has another substantial benefit. The rewards for self-reliance go beyond outstanding results and fortify your Warlock confidence – the key to leadership and self-worth, the very foundations of power.

Fearing to pursue the woman of one's dreams may not seem like the stuff that builds power, but I can tell you firsthand that it does. In my early 20s I was besotted with a beautiful co-ed who was the president of the Italian club at my college. She was also a part-time fashion model, Pilates instructor, and culinary major. What a package! She was without exaggeration a stunning classic beauty. Long, lean, and bountiful in all the right places. But she didn't date very much because most men were intimidated by her ferociously good looks.

I was no different, until I pushed past my fear of rejection and being just another name on the list of suitors who bit the dust. I threw caution to the wind, said what the hell, tapped into my Satanic moxie, and asked her on a date. And no, she didn't turn me into a newt. She said yes, but the date itself was prefaced by sweaty hands, pounding heart, and every possible OCD disaster I could dream up. The girl was wonderful, the date went great, and we were a serious item for many months. And that was some of the most incredible boot knocking of my life!

But there was no happily ever after. You see, she was so gorgeous that every time we were out in public, so many men would hit on her that I'd always end up in a fight. This got so out of hand that eventually we broke up over it. Ahhh, but I think of her to this day, and know that I succeeded because I seized my power and zigged toward the unknown instead of zagging to safety, as my more cautious self would have preferred.

MAGIC AND POWER

The practice of Lesser and Greater Magic are themselves tools of power for the Warlock seeking control over his life. By understanding the proven key elements of achieving power and applying them to his workings, the Warlock "sets the stage" for the results in accordance with his own will.

What follows are the proven pathways to power, time-tested by the very rich, the very famous, and almost always the most deliciously decadent!

THE SIX SATANIC LAWS OF POWER

If Satan really had a calling card, it would undoubtedly read "Seducer extraordinaire – congenial yet cunning, democratic yet devious." Use charm, seduction, deception, subversion, misdirection, and the practice of Lesser and Greater magic to secure power for yourself. When seeking power, make no bones about it; you are at war. Remain civilized, but deadly serious. Wield your sword with a smile on your face.

"As Satanists, we know one of the keys to success is an unflinching belief that there are no rules. Anyone who's ever succeeded has gone on that premise; not buying established procedures, business or otherwise. The naysayers are inevitably left behind amid shouts of 'it cannot be done' and 'should not be done.'" –Anton Szandor LaVey, *Satan Speaks!*

LAW 1. SEDUCE

"Seduction is foreplay to power."

Like the mating game, seduction is the first step in winning over any person or situation. Chapter 6 is devoted to this subject alone and is the longest chapter in this book because seduction is central to everything the Warlock does. No matter his Archetype, the Warlock must use his charm to set himself apart from the crowd.

• The powerful always look unique. It may be very subtle, but something about the appearance is always remembered. Use your dark persona – develop an aura of mystery and you'll wield the essence of "evil." Reinvent yourself to suit your situation. Be a showman and create dazzling spectacles for people to remember and talk about for years to come.

• See yourself as Satan himself – the grand monarch of Hell! Belief in your infernal birthright will let you carry yourself as a monarch. Your confidence will win you the crown and others will treat you like royalty (instead of giving you the royal treatment).

• Make people who can promote your goals see your value. Identify and solve their problems so they know their happiness came from you. But (like the Godfather) don't make them completely independent: while they're under your spell they will willingly do your bidding.

• Indulge people's fantasies whenever you can. They will welcome you as a larger-than-life magician, bringing pleasure and liberating them from their mundane lives. Provide the missing romance they crave.

• Charm people's hearts and minds. Trying to coerce them into thinking your way only creates a backlash. Instead, compliment their strengths and downplay their weaknesses. Help them identify their fears and create real solutions and you will have their eternal gratitude.

• Make everything look easy and natural. Panic only advertises weakness. Keep a cool head and rely on your best tricks (and members of your support team) to overcome obstacles. Surround yourself with strong lieutenants. "Never let them see you sweat." When the maelstrom around you is at a boil, make your enemies look frazzled in comparison.

• Guard your reputation with your life. Reputation defines status and is the cornerstone of power. You will be known by your reputation and, as it strengthens so will your opportunities to expand your power.

• "Fake it 'til you make it." Don't be a poseur, but do accentuate your strong points in conversation and action, always acting like you have the goods to close the deal.

• Do not accept free favors if they make you seem unable to fend for yourself. Always pay your own way and be overly generous, especially with other powerful people.

LAW 2. BE INVISIBLE

"The finest trick of the devil is to persuade you that he does not exist." – Charles Baudelaire, "Le Joueur généreux," *Le Spleen de Paris*

"Never let them see you coming." – Al Pacino in "The Devil's Advocate"

• When your intentions and strategies are too well known, you become predictable and ordinary – the antithesis of power. Stay diabolically in the shadows. Your enemies can't prepare for your next move if they don't know it.

• Miss a select few gatherings or meetings to create an air of scarcity and increase your value. People will work harder to earn your attendance because functions you attend are always more famous (or infamous).

• Be a shapeshifter. Mimic the posture, language, and stance of your enemies, flattering them into thinking you want to be like them. This manipulation of their unconscious will disarm them, leaving them much more receptive to your agenda.

• When jockeying for position, never outperform insecure superiors. Displaying your superior talents to an unconfident higher-up will only make you his target. Be a sly devil and do as the courtiers did; bow until the time is right to strike. Serve your unstable master well and make him feel god-like whenever you can. Please him and you live to learn from him another day, until his sun sets and yours rises.

LAW 3. BE CUNNING

"There is a beast in man that should be exercised, not exorcised." Anton Szandor LaVey

Like the wolf, the Warlock must call on the cunning of his inner beast to obtain what he desires.

• Be mysteriously vague in your words and actions. Say less, not more.

• Don't put too much trust in people too quickly, as many will turn on you out of envy or jealousy.

• Keep your enemies close and, when possible, use former enemies against them.

• Use your minions to do hard tasks. Acknowledge their efforts but make sure everyone knows the idea was yours. You are the general and they your foot soldiers.

• Never take sides or commit too quickly to a cause other than yourself. Allow others to persuade you and don't rush to judgment.

• Don't blame others for your visible mistakes, and don't dwell on them either. Taking responsibility for your actions (whatever the outcome) shows great leadership.

• Provide options but stack the deck in your favor so others can think doing what you want is their decision.

• Fools will never understand the intricacies of your plans. But beware

the clever underling on the rise; you were once him.
- Avoid those who portray themselves as weak or overly virtuous. Real weakness would never be flaunted. Keep your eyes open to avoid falling into someone's trap.
- Beware of lavish flattery, especially from romantic partners looking to play you for a sucker.

LAW 4. APPEAR HUMBLE AND MAGNANIMOUS

"When stepped on, the worm curls up. That is a clever thing to do. Thus it re-duces its chances of being stepped on again. In the language of morality: humility."
– Friedrich Nietzsche, *"Maxims and Arrows," Twilight of the Idols*

Humility has often been the Devil's clandestine game. Bragging is off-putting to most, but letting actions speak for themselves conveys un-derlying confidence and true power.
- Be honest and sincere, but never let your guard down.
- When dealing with your enemy, offer friendship to gain access. Once his guard is down, use your foe's weaknesses and emotions against him.
- Mingle as "one of the crowd" to gather information. Know when to draw attention to yourself and when to blend in.
- Don't offend those already in power.
- Never assume you know how someone will react.
- Socialize with the successful.
- Act naïve to make enemies underestimate you.
- Surrender when there's no chance you will prevail. Admit the better man has won – for now.
- Never try to impersonate someone greater than you. It requires twice the skill and you've accomplished nothing. Be unique and original.
- Acknowledge your minor flaws with humor, not self-pity. Expecting people to think you're perfect is arrogant and makes you look like a buffoon. Never verbalize your true weaknesses or shortcomings to those who may use them against you later.

LAW 5. TAKE CHARGE

Lead us into temptation! Most people are sheep, cringing at making decisions and begging to be led. The powerful lead.

• Take calculated risks. Nothing worth having is won in safety. Fortune favors the bold.

• Timing and planning are everything. Be patient. Thoroughly analyze and strategize before making a move.

• Play with (metaphorical) fire to thrill yourself and show courage to others.

• Create the magical "cult of you" by celebrating your rising status in the hierarchies in which you are involved.

• Secure a band of followers who look up to and rely on you.

• Be the master of misdirection so your enemies and those who blindly follow them can't analyze or anticipate your moves.

• Be bold, not indecisive nor timid. When in doubt, pause and analyze; then act.

• Always do more than is asked of you because this demonstrates leadership.

• Don't argue; make your point and walk away.

• Reward productive minions and punish slackers.

• Finish what you start; leaving things half done shows a weak mind and lack of follow-through.

• Initiate big changes in small increments. Improve on the old ways but do it slowly enough that you don't create discomfort. Make sure your changes are an improvement over the previous system.

• Don't believe or immediately accept deals; be cynical and skeptical and maintain veto power until you are satisfied with your research. Then accept with confidence.

• Embrace unavoidable chaos and channel its patterns to your advantage. Think around obstacles.

LAW 6. BE MERCILESS

"Make yourself sheep and the wolves will eat you." – Benjamin Franklin
"Hate your enemies with a whole heart, and if a man smite you on

the cheek, SMASH him on the other! Smite him hip and thigh, for self-preservation is the highest law." – The Book of Satan: 3:7.

• Totally crush your enemies in mind and spirit. Make examples of vanquished enemies for others to fear. Do not stop halfway. Do not negotiate.

• Identify the leader of a group of adversaries and eliminate him/her. Without the alpha wolf, the rival pack will scatter.

• Acknowledging your enemies transfers your power to them; don't do it.

• Beware the overly meek and call the phonies on their ploy before they can strike. Those who advertise innocence are often the least innocent.

• Use the rumored power and mystique of the dark arts to their fullest. Use your mastery of magic and the occult to frighten and mystify those who would do you harm.

• Challenge bullies *mano a mano*. Most will back down.

• Call on Satan to do your bidding in the presence of those who are not Satanists, then laugh as they cower at the very sound of His name.

warlock wisdom

- Power is the Devil's game; it satisfies all that we lust after.

- Real power lies within your control.

- Lesser and Greater Magic are important tools and means to power.

- Exploit your Warlock persona as a symbol of your mystery and power.

- Know that most people (including friends and relatives) may at times try to hurt you out of envy or jealousy.

- Self-confidence gives you the power to face all circumstances.

- Be cunning. Anticipate a foe's next move.

- Be invisible. Never let them see you coming.

- Seduction is foreplay to power.

- Beware romantic and lavish flattery. We are all suckers when it comes to our egos. Witches entice us with beauty and stroke our egos. Recognize this fact and enjoy the ride.

- Facing fear creates power in all circumstances and forces you to constantly step up your game.

more

warlock wisdom

- Be bold, fluid, and unconventional. Create a spectacle when required.

- Embrace chaos and channel its patterns to your advantage.

- Don't avoid problems; treat them as opportunities.

- Never be passive; always opt to be active and out of your comfort zone. Momentum builds confidence and impresses those around you.

- Turn negative situations to positives by seeking a new path.

- Don't dwell on failures and setbacks.

- Never verbalize your true faults or shortcomings to your adversaries.

- Show your enemies no mercy.

THE SECRET ART OF SATANIC SEDUCTION

"It is in the mind – in her fantasies – that a woman plays the mating game. Not in the loins as it is with men."

Nothing is more Satanic than seduction. Satan is the great seducer, the ultimate gentleman, the purveyor of pleasures you never see coming. As actor Al Pacino's Satan character so aptly put it in *The Devil's Advocate*, "I'm the hand up the Mona Lisa's skirt."

Seduction *absolutely* is the Devil's game. Diabolic, clandestine, and the very fuel of the mating dance. Seduction is an art, opening doors to countless delights while teaching a man to see the whole world as his bedroom. Seduction is the great leg opener, the spark of infatuation, and the stuff of romantic delirium. Its purpose is to make one lose oneself and fall in love (or at least lust). Seduction may be the precursor to longstanding relationships (or a way to sustain them), but first it must ignite the flames of desire!

So it is befitting that the core of every Satanic Warlock is his ability and expertise as the consummate carnal seducer. This is man's primary motivation and has been so since the dawn of time. Man may have left the caves, but the skills needed to close the deal haven't. Seduction, dear fellows, is all *salesmanship.*

Throughout history, the character of Satan has taken on numerous personalities and appeared in many different disguises. He first attracts, then convinces his mark to bend to his will, "selling" the mark on his power. He is often forceful but can also take a softer approach, sometimes even appearing androgynous or meek. But his goal has always been the same – to mesmerize his prey and win the day.

EMBRACE AND USE YOUR DARK IMAGE

As a Warlock and a Satanist, you already possess a certain darkness. You are the villain most people fear and yet want to be near. Your presence suggests danger and mystery. Lesser beings immediately notice and are drawn to your Satanic presence, so use it to the hilt!

Today's Warlocks face new challenges to test their mettle in the game of seduction. Social networking and instant communication have forever changed the mating ritual. Forget about slowly building your personal mystery; seduction may be over before it even begins. In bygone days, courting, dating, and teasing were all steps in a calculated dance that took days, weeks, or even months to consummate, creating many mental and physical delights for both parties [see *The Devil's Notebook* and *The Satanic Witch*]. Today all this delicious tension has been telescoped by tech and now (often regrettably), the whole arc can play out in just minutes.

Technology also brings us the "manosphere" – a virtual boot camp catering to the masses of feminized men desperate for advice. Despite the fact that society has been progressively liberal in sex and pornography, men – especially younger millennials – are still having trouble getting laid! The manosphere supports an entire industry of digital "Dear Abby"s. Young Pick Up Artists (PUAs) and seduction gurus give advice to lovelorn, besieged men trapped in what they believe is the overly restrictive framework controlling their entire lives. Although these sites offer nothing new, the rubes buying into the PUA line are shelling out big money to get a lot of nothing.

The gurus call for a rebirth of the "alpha" male, a man who won't cave in to the conditioning of the "feminine mystique." The self-proclaimed masters hawk *game* – the ability to orchestrate relationships with women, with all roads leading to the bedroom. They label millions of regular guys AFCs (for "average frustrated chumps"), preying on their frustrations. Not only does this create hostility, it turns what should be lusty and playful (and *enjoyable*) into a mean game of getting on top, both literally and figuratively. Their methods tip the scales well into the opposite extreme, often using degrading techniques in an effort to "put women in their place."

One of the cornerstones of the PUA movement, "dropping a NEG" (NEGative comment) is a devious and cowardly mind-fuck. Warlocks must be suave and never obviously insulting; these tactics are a much too hostile and crass to work on any savvy woman. Dropping the NEG is only effective with younger, insecure females (18-25), but shouldn't be used on them either. More experienced women won't tolerate men pointing out their shortcomings, and will most likely call them on their shit before dismissing them as assholes. Clever Witches will certainly see through this gambit in short order. *Intimidation isn't seduction.*

But have no fear, because the Warlock is not a PUA (and the PUA is not a Warlock). Warlocks never needed this kind of "help" because we've never fallen for political correctness. Satanism is and always will be a philosophy and religion that celebrates the *individual,* regardless of gender. This is an important distinction to understand as it allows Warlocks to execute their seduction without resorting to an overly aggressive "alpha" attack plan. We know where we stand! Unlike the insecure, hungry to demonstrate their *machismo,* Warlocks embrace their natural, instinctive masculinity. We can take many forms and play out numerous scenarios of seduction using our naturally masculine Satanic traits.

Confidence and security keep us head and shoulders above the rubes and are the basis of all techniques of seduction. We have no interest in the regurgitated hogwash peddled by an Internet cabal of twenty-something, fast-talking con men.

Which is not to say that some of the "expert" advice doesn't work. The distinction is that their "wisdom" is mostly random and unverified data, compiled from blog posts and recycled pop psychology. The same old tricks with new names – some valuable, some hotly disputed, and some just egocentric nonsense. Even a broken clock is right twice a day.

But whatever they're selling, it isn't news to the Satanic Warlock! Many Warlocks already identify as the "alpha" (LaVey's 12 o'clock position) and inherently understand that, as males and their own gods, they can affect their surroundings and create their desired results using seduction alone.

By successfully developing the Warlock Self (Chapter 3), all feelings of doubt or insecurity are neutralized, leaving the Warlock well equipped to apply the following seduction techniques. Unlike most, the Warlock is, by definition, both psychologically and sociologically geared to exercise his male traits in relationships and seduction. Warlocks *already* identify as part of a patriarchal tribe and won't buy into forced feminization. Satanism energizes and empowers both Witch and Warlock, allowing each gender to fully realize, celebrate, and *enjoy* the different roles they play in the mating game. Electricity is generated when the positives of one gender play off the negatives of the other. Creating two neutrals just yields nothing.

Not all Warlocks identify as alphas or feel driven to move towards 12 o'clock. For those who do want to step up their game, though, fasten your seatbelts.

BEWARE THE MYTH OF "WOMEN AS THE ROMANTICS"

Warlocks must understand a very important distinction between the male and female genders before embarking on the path of seduction: As Anton LaVey said in *The Satanic Witch*, men are animals first and romantics second. Once the initial hunt is over and we don't have to work to get laid, we become the romantics. WE become vulnerable, because we are driven by our fragile egos. WE are the idealistic believers in love and passion, and are completely lost without it – not women.

Our own High Priestess Peggy Nadramia said it best: "That's why men spend fortunes on elaborate sex dolls, while women just get a vibrator (many of which don't even look like penises)." The king of all vibrators is still the Hitachi Magic Wand, which is basically a tennis ball on a stick. But if the house is on fire, nine out of 10 women will grab the Hitachi and let the photo of their boyfriend burn.

This is not to say women don't love and respond to romance, but *men* need it to be "real" in order to stay mentally and physically consumed by passion and wild sex. Lust, a surge of oxytocin (the love and intimacy hormone) and limerence (being utterly spellbound by someone) initially fuel these deep desires, clouding many men's minds. Most "crimes of passion" are committed by men, not women. Conversely, no woman ever believed a male stripper was really her boyfriend. Men can't tell the difference between their purely animal sex drives and the more elevated concept of love. Our thinking brain may tell us we want mature, healthy, supportive partnerships, but our lower brains make sure we are never far from selfish egocentric cavemen. We gleefully mock women for needing to be in love to fuck, but we still need to personalize the event. We may agree with *The Satanic Bible* that lust and desire are more accurate terms to describe love "when applied to the continuance of the race," but we forget how much love matters to our egos.

WHAT FIRST ATTRACTS A WOMAN?

Needless to say, initial attraction is dependent on numerous subjective variables, especially including a woman's mood at the moment you saunter up to her. But some age-old wisdom never fails.

As noted in Chapter 3, confidence is without a doubt the first and best mating signal. Physical subtleties and non-verbal behaviors that display dominant behavior include standing your ground around other men, declarative speech, and gazing into her eyes while smiling. All of these are attractive to women. Conversely, don't fidget, slump, cross your arms across your chest, or cross your legs at the knee while seated (typically a feminine posture).

You'll know she's responding if she makes quick eye contact and then glances away, leans her body towards yours while talking, plays with her hair or jewelry, points her foot toward you, or strokes an object (like a glass or lighter) while chatting.

Should you need them (but as a Warlock you should be *paying attention*), "get the hell away from her" signals include no eye contact, checking the time, looking over your head to scan the room while talking, body language that points away from you, and of course if she actually says something like "not interested," move your ass down to the next bar stool!

NAVIGATING HER "CIRCLES OF HELL"

When men are horny they have only one goal – they want to get laid. That's about as linear as it gets. They see something they like, create a fantasy, then turn on the charm and hope she goes for it.

But women approach the mating game much differently. Metaphorically speaking, they put men through their "Circles of Hell" often confusing and frustrating men until they successfully navigate each circle. A woman may be attracted to a man, but her first impulse isn't to wonder how his cock will taste. The idea may be in the back of her mind, but she sees seduction as a marathon, not a sprint.

For a Warlock to be successful at seduction, he must realize it is not the "point A to point B" that exists in his head. Women use circular thinking, not linear thinking. A woman may feel a strong physical attraction but, except in cases where she too just wants a bit of the old in-out, her mind will first seek validation on other levels. She'll wonder if he pays his bills, is up to his eyeballs in debt, or if he owns or rents. She may indeed be enjoying the idea of his body next to hers, but then suddenly wonder if he's allergic to cats (or worse, hates them). A woman's selection process is more sophisticated and much less visually dependent than a man's. She's horny, but she's still sizing him up to gauge how he will treat her *after* he gets his rocks off. There's no predictable progression of thought while she weighs physical attraction against her emotional needs.

The savvy Warlock must understand this and follow her lead. Don't feel you're losing the battle if her interest seems to cool or shift gears. As noted, the game is in her mind and her mind has a lot more moving parts than a man's. The signals in men's heads (both of them) are much simpler. All men really get is: "Hot body! Let's fuck!"

The Warlock must not become frustrated when she asks questions that seem to have nothing to do with seduction (and there can be many). Know that each question is a test, so make the answers personal to her. For example, if she interrupts heated flirting to ask about your career, don't just say, "I'm a marine biologist." Instead, mention some of your achievements and invite her to visit your workplace,

Navigating her "CIRCLES OF HELL"

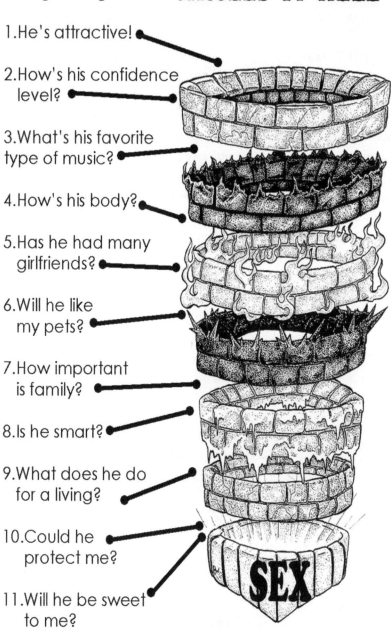

1. He's attractive!

2. How's his confidence level?

3. What's his favorite type of music?

4. How's his body?

5. Has he had many girlfriends?

6. Will he like my pets?

7. How important is family?

8. Is he smart?

9. What does he do for a living?

10. Could he protect me?

11. Will he be sweet to me?

SEX

or show her something you've created. The art here is to help her successfully vet you and convince her that you're trustworthy (a bell-wether for the sex to come). The sooner a man satisfies her "circles," the closer he gets to her bed. Once this is accomplished, seduction moves into high gear.

GET RHYTHM

Human bodies are rhythmic. Warlocks must never discount the effect hormones play on women. Those lovely bodies run on a some-times volatile cocktail of estrogen, progesterone, and testosterone. Research finds that a man's attractiveness varies significantly depending on which hormones are in play. For example, women are attracted to alpha men when they're ovulating (their estrogen is peaking), because at that time they're looking for someone to protect them and make healthy babies. Softer beta men are only on their radar during the second two weeks of the cycle (progesterone peaking). The ladies tend to be more irritable and looking for comfort, so betas are much more likely to fit the bill. These cycles fluctuate as women get older and enter perimenopause and menopause (40s – 50s), when reproduction is no longer a motivator and more varied mood swings are common.

Testosterone, the male hormone that peaks in adolescence and early adulthood and usually makes men much hornier (10 to 100 times more), also plays an important part in female behavior. Women's levels peak in their 30s, so a 20-year-old man and 30-year-old-woman are often the best fit sexually. The levels are compatible again later in life, when testosterone drops off for both men and women.

How does this help a Warlock succeed at seduction? Since (biologically speaking) sex is about baby-making, it should be obvious that women are more apt to want sex when they're ovulating. Men don't usually need to see their calendars; they subconsciously pick up on the signals. Many strippers have confided that they make better tips when ovulating. They feel sexier and the guys respond! Make the effort to learn and pay attention to your target's entire cycle (not just when she's "on the rag") and act accordingly.

THE POWER OF LUST

Lust is, of course, the cornerstone of our carnal religion. Almost all other religions call it a sin (sometimes a deadly one!), but lust must be recognized as the Warlock's most trusted ally. Lust is part and parcel to the Law of the Forbidden because it drives our most secret curiosities:

What's under that dress? How might those panties taste?

Dante's *Inferno* assigns Lust to one of the Nine Circles of Hell (So it must be fun!). He defined lust as the "excessive love of others," a sin because it rivaled and surpassed the love of God. God may have no meaning to a Satanist, but you get the point.

Lust motivates us to pursue pleasure. When a woman catches your eye, mentally absorb what it is about her that sets you aflame. Most likely it will be a part of her anatomy. If it's her large breasts, create the scenario in your mind of kneading her flesh, flicking the nipples into hardness and sucking and biting every inch. If you're an ass man, picture her on all fours, inviting you to grab her full buttocks and spreading her cheeks wide, just for you. Your lust is powerful. Let it consume you. Feel your erection becoming engorged. This fire gives you the strength and courage to move forward. In many cases your lust can create a pheromone response in the woman you desire.

Deconstructing and understanding lust would take a far more involved study, but for the purpose of seduction, the Warlock needs to understand its simplest definition – and its power! In a 1998 paper, Helen Fisher Ph.D, a biological anthropologist and senior research fellow at the famous Kinsey Institute, described lust as one of three stages of how we choose mates (along with attraction and attachment). Lust is testosterone-driven (much higher in males than females), meaning Warlocks must isolate and employ lust as their prime mover. All else will (or won't) fall into place, depending on how a woman reacts.

The word lust gets a bad rap from people who think all it does is fuel man's basest desires. But research into its origins (not surprisingly) find lust being demonized only by religious prudery. Everyone else recognizes its ability to deliver both physical and emotional gratification. Religious adherents call lust selfish and narcissistic because they fear sexual pleasure and don't want anyone else to have any either.

Lust serves as the catalyst for a Warlock's ECI, unleashing and reflecting his most animalistic instincts. With his id unchained, the Warlock is liberated from the self-censoring super-ego (normally a moral watchdog). Herein lies the magical power. Identify your lust – feel it and embrace it when approaching a situation or potential mate, and it will carry you across the finish line every time.

Lust is also "desire," which motivates the woman you want to seduce. According to researcher Emily Nagoski in her book on female sexuality, *Come As You Are: The Surprising New Science That Will Transform Your Sex Life*, women will respond to your seduction (let you fuck them) only if the context is right. Women need to be in the proper mood and are often less spontaneous about having sex than men (men: 75 percent, women: 10 percent). That means the Warlock must be aware of the circumstances during the seduction. Humans have sexual "accelerators" and "brakes" to initiate, move, and stop sexual excitement. A woman's accelerator has a lot of qualifiers – is she sufficiently turned on, is the location safe, will this guy have any idea how to operate (or even find) her clitoris…?

As a diabolical Warlock, you must control the process by asking questions and setting the mood. Her accelerator could be pressed by a touch or soft word. Check in with her. Ask her how she feels, particularly if an intoxicant is involved. When you get the go sign, ignite and harness lust to drive yourself and satisfy her desires.

THE MEPHISTO WALTZ OR THE ART OF SATANIC SEDUCTION

Moving forward, we assume the Warlock is proficient in both Lesser and Greater magic. What follows can be used as spur-of-the-moment stand-alone techniques to bewitch the object of his desire.

When beginning seduction, the Warlock must suspend normal moral constraints. He must understand that seduction is like a war (Winning is everything!) and use all the weapons in his arsenal to prevail. He must understand what makes him seductive (his Archetype Self) and know what will make his intended surrender to his advances. Focusing on the Self without knowing your target's needs – her need for romance or to be freed from a bad relationship – is a fatal error. But when these elements combine, your spell is cast!

The Warlock can choose from a multitude of seduction techniques, many tried and true for centuries by great seducers, both real and fictional. They combine the dark forces of our animal nature with our Satanic orthodoxy, intensifying both. Use this undefiled wisdom to bolster your romantic repertoire!

SEDUCTION IN THE DIGITAL AGE

The Internet and new dating and hook-up apps that themselves breed like rabbits have made it almost impossible to seduce from a distance any more. Opinions vary; the new way can be a fiery accelerant and facilitate a doubly hot sexual encounter or a total short-circuit.

Removing the face-to-face human factor from the selection process may actually make tech-happy men forget the art of real life seduction, relying instead on shortcuts promising immediate gratification. Dirty texts, meat market apps, and Facetime can't replace the myriad nuances, whispers, touches, gazes, and more that comprise genuine (and I might add, much more stimulating) seduction. Give me a wink and an eyebrow raise over an emoticon any day!

A 2015 *Vanity Fair* article about the Tinder hook-up app pointed out that although many younger women are indeed enjoying multiple sex partners without the "slut-shaming" of the past, most still want to land a traditional monogamous boyfriend once they've had their sexual fill. The guys, however, keep on hunting and gathering. Man sprays his seed and woman feathers her nest.

What's more, much of the Warlock's mysterious persona – his stock in trade – is completely lost in digital transmission. Real seduction requires more than 72 pixels per inch. Can a webcam capture the Warlock's smoldering in-person *kavorka*? So much more sexual stimulus and intrigue happen in a face-to-face meeting, fueled by swirling pheromones and the chemistry between the partners. The apps may be fun at first, but instant gratification eventually leads to boredom.

And despite nearly everyone using technology (no more social stigma around "having" to resort to online dating), most men never mention how often they get rejected. Virtual rejections *should* only cause minor disappointment, but in truth this kind of grand-scale negativity deflates confidence and erodes the humanity of a generation already built on entitlement. Victory in seduction is so much sweeter when it employs the Warlock's entire personal arsenal – not just his thumbs.

THE IMPORTANCE (?) OF PHYSICAL ATTRACTIVENESS

As discussed in Chapter 3, a man's physical attractiveness is important in seduction – but not for the reasons you used to think. Women may be less visually motivated, but most of them aren't blind. Looks still matter (sorry fellas) – particularly if you've given up on them. The handsomer Warlock may have a better chance of catching a woman's eye, but the deal is sealed by how he embodies his Archetype. There's no mystery here. There are of course exceptions – fame, money and power are all trump cards (see the Satanic *Masculinity Meter* on page 153 for a reality check) – but for the typical Warlock (or any man) decent looks and a healthy physique are just the jumping off point.

… Meaning all is not lost for the non-Adonis Warlock. Like the Witch, if traditional beauty isn't an option, a unique style (your Archetype) will still spark the command to look, activating sex, sentiment, and wonder to facilitate your Lesser Magic. Regardless of the accuracy of the statement, the Warlock must believe he is the sexiest man ever born.

Some things can't change. He can't get taller, but the motivated Warlock can overcome a preponderance of merely physical shortcomings with commitments to making himself otherwise valuable. Learn to cook, get into passable (or even excellent) shape, play an instrument or sing, and, of course, pay meticulous attention to grooming. Women want their brains stimulated along with their naughty bits. Be the man they can brag about to their friends.

It takes hard work and dedication to your Archetype, but every milestone builds confidence. The Warlock should also take a page from *The Satanic Witch* and learn to flaunt his best attributes (not just adopt new ones). Is your hair long and flowing? Many women are entranced by long hair. Let them brush it! Be ready for this – keep it clean and perfectly conditioned. Deep green eyes, flecked with gold? Wear something emerald green (earring, scarf or necktie) to show your style and bring out their color. Create your personal style, scent, and mannerisms. Maybe even adopt an exotic accent. But remember, when the clothes come off, you'll still need to deliver the goods!

The muscle man gets attention from women not so much for the bulge of his arms or the broadness of his chest, but because his girth represent *security* – the strength to fend off predators and keep his woman safe. But we've moved out of caves, and if his brawn isn't backed up by character, her interest will wane. A woman may only notice the hours you've spent on your pecs in a casual post-coital glance.

Above all, remember that positives and negatives about your looks exist only in your mind. Never allow a negative self-image to undermine and poison your confidence. Every person will judge you differently based on what he or she considers appealing. For every one woman who's turned off by your acne scars, there are a dozen who'd love to hear more about your pilot's license, your charity work with animals, the five languages you speak, or your lifelong study of astronomy. It cannot be overstressed that intriguing, confident, and seductive energy almost always trumps looks because they can be sustained.

And please NEVER use your shortcomings to get sympathy. It is weak and there's no future in it. Humility is one thing, but whining about your faults will reinforce them in your mind and drive away all but the kind of women who need a broken man.

WHAT WITCHES ARE SAYING

Don't believe that? We asked!

– *Physical attraction is only important when it's not there. I don't need to be aroused by my friends and peers, but I certainly do need to be visually and sexually captivated by my romantic partner.*

— Physical attractiveness is subjective and rather low on my importance scale. Don't get me wrong, I recognize and very much appreciate a hot body and a pretty face, but when it comes to real attraction, well, all the hotness in the world can be canceled out by stupidity very easily.

— A good personality makes you more attractive. I'm much more attracted to people based on their intelligence and manners rather than their physical being. However, people who do not take into account their physical appearance are a turn off. If you are not bathed or are morbidly obese, I lose respect.

— A true Satanic Warlock can have sex appeal and be very attractive even though his physique may not be to my liking. He will work with his physical type rather than trying to change it.

— Both women and men respond more favorably to attractive things and people. That's not to say a Warlock needs to look like he just stepped off the pages of a fashion magazine, or that there is one unifying standard of male beauty. However, a man should find a grooming and exercise regimen, as well as style of dress, that works best for him and the image he wishes to project.

— Women have a much broader sense of physical attraction than men do. Most men are brainwashed by media and salivate like dogs at any pre-packaged, pre-digested hottie du jour.

— Maybe because women aren't spoon-fed what is supposed to be attractive, or maybe because women have evolved as different creatures, women truly do find a wider range of man physically attractive. It has been said that a man is attracted to symmetry, youthfulness, and vigor in a woman because he is hardwired to look for a woman to pass along robust, healthy genes to his offspring. He also seeks variety for evolutionary needs. On the other hand, women are looking for power — not necessarily muscles, but a confidence and commanding presence that communicates strength and surety, meaning security for her and her offspring.

— The best approach a Satanic Warlock can take is to work with what he has. No matter what your shape, be confident, and cultivate whatever practical skills you can — music is always charming, art, cooking, working with wood or metal, something demonstrable you can take pride in. Don't be afraid to be a little silly and vulnerable sometimes — these moments give a woman the feeling she's getting to know the real you (true or not). Physical attractiveness comes from how closely you match up with her particular ECI and how sure you feel in your own being. That, fortunately for most men, can have a broad range of physical expressions. Just as Dr. LaVey identified in The Satanic Witch, *express yourself in the context of sex, sentiment and wonder, or a combination of those, and you will be hard to resist.*

BECOMING THE SEDUCER – AROUSING THE FERAL URGE

The Warlock must access and stimulate a woman's mind in order to bring her feral urge to the surface. He does this by discovering what motivates and excites her, what sets her wild imaginings on fire. This is how and where he establishes his foothold in her inner world, her imagination, her fantasies.

Despite their conscious use of "bitchcraft," when it comes to choosing their mates, women operate on a largely unconscious level – motivated by biology and fixed psychological patterns. The Warlock must stage his seduction in this deep area of a woman's psyche.

As LaVey's ECI explains, men's fetishes are often the result of seeing specific women's items they then associate with their first sexual experience or awakening. Following his observations, women also have ECI/vanity/ego triggers, albeit more subtle and cerebral. Whereas men get turned on by things like stockings, panties, or certain hair colors and body parts, women's fetishes often center on the less concrete (things that manifest in their minds, not their hands) like odors and sensations. LaVey also discussed this, citing touch, music, and the creation of a beautiful, safe world in which everything is about her.

Your target is a combination of her ECI and the time in her life when she was most emotional and romantically impressionable (usually adolescence to early 20s). Many women love music or art, developing deep-seated romantic fantasies tied to favorite artists or musicians. In the old days, girls cut actual pictures out of magazines and tried on the last names of their movie star or musician "boyfriends." Today it's digital, but it's still the same process. The clever Warlock will ask about her childhood interests (itself a tool of seduction), learning everything he can. If he doesn't fit the bill personally (not being the painter or singer or actor she longed for as a teen), he must find ways to incorporate the passion itself into their shared moments. LaVey's observations about music validate this concept. He wrote that if you want to please someone, it helps to use the kind of music closest to that person's position on the Synthesizer Clock. This groundwork is the first step to awakening her feral urge.

Once you find out what she likes, showering your intended with gifts is another tried-and-true tactic. Small thoughtful gifts are perfect, as long as whatever you give lets her know you've been listening. It really is the thought that counts. If your woman loves Emily Dickinson's poetry, don't just order a book from Amazon and ship it to her post office box. Instead, print out her favorite poem, frame it, wrap it, and have it hand delivered (preferably to her office, so all the other women can see). If she's a foodie, don't settle for date night at your local Denny's because it's halfway between her place and yours; splurge and leave your comfort zone. Take her to a ridiculously fancy restaurant (like Boston's Legal Seafoods, or Hollywood's Musso and Frank) for no real reason at all. Take great pride in the lengths you are willing to go to to impress and delight her.

USE PLEASURE AS A WEAPON

Pleasure is the Warlock's most diabolic weapon. He delivers not just physical (sexual) pleasure, but also the emotional pleasure a woman gets when he replaces life's insecurity with his unique combination of mystery and stability. Feeding her head and heart is as pleasurable to her as sucking her clit, as it plays into her Prince Charming fantasy and creates a sense of well-being. When she thinks the Warlock can provide whatever she needs, she will find him irresistible. Most women are thrilled to have a strong, exciting Warlock lead them astray.

NEITHER A NICE GUY NOR AN ASSHOLE BE

The Warlock knows seduction often involves roleplaying. But if there is one role a Warlock must not play in the initial stages of seduction, it's that of non-threatening platonic good-guy friend. Not only is creating a fake non-threatening persona to "accidentally" get into a girl's pants dishonest and desperate, eventually she's going to find out it was a ruse. Don't be a wolf in sheep's clothing! The would-be Warlock whose strategy displays overt and fawning femininity and puppy dog loyalty will be disappointed – this tactic is not only not sexy, it will probably backfire. This kind of posturing screams *weakness* to most women, if not openly, then certainly on an unconscious level. Women are genetically and sociologically geared to want sex with men who are confident leaders, not mushy pals. Learn CPR with her (you could save her life), but don't volunteer to drive her neighbor to the airport at 3am when you live more than an hour away. The misguided male who thinks he's showing "boyfriend material" by being overly accommodating and letting a woman take advantage is setting himself up for disaster. Women biologically and psychologically don't respect (and won't sleep with) men they think of as doormats – despite what they say they want. Men have been buying into the feminist lie that women want "sensitive" men for too long.

This of course is not to mean you shouldn't be sincere or a gentleman. A Warlock treats women with respect, admiration, and appreciation. What we are addressing here are the *beginning stages of seduction* where the goal is to spark a romance with the intent to get laid. Let's not kid ourselves; most men are hunting for sex from the get-go. A relationship may develop as desires and expectations change. But initially, the man's market value – his ability to show leadership, confidence, fearlessness, and strength, along with some level of physical attractiveness – is what sparks the woman he desires, wins her attention, and sets the stage for sex.

There's a danger in the early part of a relationship. If you appear to care too much a girl may back away. She may often be more attracted to somebody who she thinks is hard to get – just as a guy often is. Of course there is nothing rational about that. As a matter of fact, it's counterproductive. But it's a reality. Unfortunately, it then becomes a game, which means you have to sometimes hold back your true feelings to keep her from running away." – Hugh Hefner, *Hef's Little Black Book*

The overly nice "nice guy" is a character created out of fear: fear of rejection, low self-esteem about physical shortcomings, fear of being alone, or being criticized by peers. Warlocks are not herd animals. Face your fears and forge your own Satanic, confident path. You'll never close the deal without it!

THE WARLOCK AS THE PRIZE OR THE CAT AND STRING APPROACH

"Discover a lady in trouble; be attentive; extricate her from her difficulty; bestow small gifts; use alluring words; make hay; get bored; exit stage left." – Casanova.

One of the first orders of business in the art of seduction is turning the tables on the traditional thinking that the woman is the only prize to be won. Women have become opportunistic creatures in the game of love. Women decide if a man has the right stuff to gain entry to their lives (and beds). Their clever gamesmanship casually dangles the carrot (sex) in front of the man, enjoying the show as he dutifully chases it. Many men have succumbed to the idea that if they want pussy they must first prove themselves worthy. As Satanic Witches are well aware, there's little skill needed to make men dance like puppets.

The Warlock must recognize this approach and enjoy it for the challenge and the ultimate pleasure it promises! But he must also remember that HE might also be the prize! As counter-intuitive as this may seem (usually as a result of women putting men through their paces before they surrender the goods), the Warlock should first seem captivated by her charms by spinning a web of romantic words and gestures until she is equally mesmerized … and then back off to initiate the tease. This creates the "cat and string" or "chase/be chased" scenario. Despite what they say, most women abhor a man they find predictable. The sometimes infuriating game of tease and retreat keeps her off-guard and intrigued. This often works best when the woman thinks the Warlock has little interest in her. The idea that she's no longer the object of his desire will vex her and make her want him all the more.

Women have been playing this game for centuries. But Warlocks have the same power – maybe more, because ins and outs of seduction are played in the mind of a woman.

Create sexual tension; the to and fro will set the stage for a deliciously erotic release. Occasionally show strategic minor weakness to suggest your feminine side (an inner need for most women). Don't be a broken record of masculine clichés – fast cars, cigars, dark clothes, and gruff demeanor. Also show her something of your feminine side. Many men call the color red (for clothing or cars) "girl's choice," but red attracts women like moths to flame. Choosing red shows them something they already like and suggests you have a softer side, making you doubly appealing.

Give uncommon and unexpected gifts. Aim for her "love trigger" with a gift from your heart. Skip the diamond bracelet and buy her dog that collar she swoons over every time she's in the pet store. Women melt when they know you are listening, and we all know the devil is in the details.

What needs to be emphasized here is the importance of *patience* (more on this later). Men, as natural fixers and problem solvers are often very impatient about getting results, both from everyday tasks and gaining the affection of someone they desire. But patience – the ability to set and follow a plan, then follow it and wait for the outcome – is essential in seduction. Women are in no hurry. They would rather build the scenario in their minds, savor it, and fantasize about the outcome rather than immediately "get busy."

Granted, this waiting for a response can be maddening to men. Especially when a Warlock's desire is focused on one woman. This is why dating a few women is ideal. The manosphere calls this "spinning plates," and it definitely relieves some of the tension.

By being patient and not forcing the issue, the Warlock appears sexy, cool, and confident (instead of desperate), increasing his value in a woman's mind. This is a powerful tool. But if there is no response after three attempts, move on to another woman. No need to force the issue when there are plenty of fish in the sea.

WORDS ARE DIABOLICAL

Language is a potent weapon in every aspect of seduction. Words evoke powerful emotions and leave long-lasting impressions in the mind of the person being seduced. Think about a situation where you or someone you know has been called stupid, asshole, ugly, fat, or some other derogatory term. Now think about a heartfelt compliment acknowledging beauty, intelligence, or some other ego-gratifying trait. Words are like music – good and bad, they get under the skin. Know that your words will have staying power and say things you know will please.

Despite a Warlock's natural masculine leanings, soft words can be valuable, both as tools and weapons. The "soft sell" is very effective as it sets the stage for your charisma to take over. Initially create enchantment, not just lust. A woman enchanted will surrender.

In fact, charisma – the combination of physical attractiveness, moderate extroversion, social ability, interpersonal skills, reliability, and of course self-confidence – requires a good dose of verbal ability.

Flattery and promises create the landscape of possibility in the mind. Suggest possibilities but don't be specific. Say us and we instead of *you* or *me*. Remember, you are building a fantasy to create desire in her mind. You must whisk her away from her mundane day-to-day reality, replacing it with your new romantic world. Use "boomerang" words whenever possible, i.e. repeat key words or phrases she uses in conversation. If she says the word "splendid" often, work that word into the conversation to show her you were listening to her and share her way of thinking.

But there's more to it than vocabulary. Your delivery is equally as important. Speak softly with an underlying sexiness when romantic, forceful when dominant (don't be afraid of dirty talk), and always be sure of what you're saying. Never worry that you're asking too many questions; everyone's favorite subject is him or herself.

THE DARK MAGIC OF NEURO-LINGUISTIC PROGRAMMING

Neuro-Linguistic Programming (NLP) is the attempt to change the internal workings of the mind through hidden, embedded commands that signify trust and intimacy. It is a staple of many of the new seduction and pickup paradigms. NLP's "process language" is a method of talking to people (covertly commanding them) by making them think the ideas are coming from them and not you. Sales people do it all the time. Politicians and religious leaders all do it too. Most people don't realize that phrases and words, when coupled with tonality and pauses can create mini-trances.

NLP was created and gained popularity through the work of Richard Bandler and other mental health practitioners. Some of the better-known NLP practitioners are Dr. Milton Erickson with Conversational Hypnosis, Dr. Fritz Perls with Gestalt Therapy, and Virginia Satir with Family Therapy.

Although the use of NLP can be considered nefarious and should be used with caution, it is worthwhile to mention that its application can be particularly effective when used in the mating game. All seduction techniques really just guide a possibly willing partner toward an idea, allowing them to want sex with you instead of others.

Warlock G. Edwin Taylor explains how NLP works through Anchoring and Triggering:

You can set up an anchor by attaching it to a feeling or emotional state. You can even anchor a thought. When you want that particular feeling, you just trigger off the anchor.

In seduction, if you get someone to feel joy, you can anchor that feeling to yourself. You can use a gesture, a word, or a touch as your anchor. Then later, you trigger off that feeling by saying that word, or doing that gesture; whatever you originally chose as your anchor. "I once had an ex-girlfriend vividly recall the feeling of an intense orgasm, which I then anchored to a particular word that I chose. Whenever I said that word, it would trigger off an amazing orgasm in her. We had fun with that one for months."

Here's an example of creating an Anchor:

"Do you remember that one time in your life when you felt truly ecstatic; that moment where you were the happiest you can be because of what was happening right in front of you and you just couldn't control your excitement? It was like you were about to burst because there you are feeling absolutely happy, right?"

(If you talk with your hands, it's easy to quickly point at yourself when you mention happy, ecstatic, etc. The split-second point happens so fast, and your hands are moving anyway, so they won't consciously notice you've anchored that happy feeling they have to you.)

And smiling while pointing to yourself extremely quickly when you say, "was happening right in front of you," well, I'm sure you get the idea.

You can't just launch into your spiel though. You need to establish a rapport first. And if your pointing or whatever is too obvious, they'll resist. First you must build rapport, by matching and mirroring their movements, breathing patterns, and body language. LaVey talked about that in *The Satanic Witch*.

Magister Nemo is also an expert, and offers these examples of NLP command words and phrases:

PHRASE OPENERS:

Imagine	WORDS:
Go to	Temptation
Believe	Pleasure
When you	Decadent
Find yourself	Feel good
Suddenly	Sensuous
Have you ever?	Delicious
As you feel	Sweet

Sentence example: *Have you ever wondered* about the real definition of evil and if temptation is what it is all about?

Examples of words that create rapport:

This/that connection
Feel how close
You don't have to (suggests empathy)
You really shouldn't

Saying any of these while casually gesturing with your hands between them and yourself should feel natural and won't draw attention to what you're doing.

MIRRORING

To establish deep rapport you need to also mirror subtle but primal behaviors in the other person. One way is to breathe in the same rhythm, or alter your stance to match theirs. If they lean to one side, you mirror that lean. Try blinking your eyes when they blink theirs. Subtly match their body motions (hand movements or head tilting) or try to match their conversational speed. If they talk fast, you should too.

To test the method, Warlocks can change a behavior and see if his target follows. Repeatedly touch your ear. If your target does the same you've established mirroring. On a preconscious level you have established rapport, and on a deep level the below-language part of their mind sees you as "part of them." Your target can now be led to more comfortable, relaxed thoughts and feelings. This is the first critical stage to reduce and remove the "uptight" emotions that prevent your target from turning her thoughts to sex. You have put her in *your trance.*

PHYSICAL STEPS TO INTIMACY

Touching and talking are powerful rapport building tools. In *The Naked Ape*, zoologist Desmond Morris presents careful studies of both apes and humans that found 12 progressive physical steps that, when followed in a fixed order, result in sex. Here are the 12 steps in order:

1. Eye to body
2. Eye to eye
3. Voice to voice (talk)
4. Hand to hand
5. Arm to shoulder
6. Arm to waist
7. Mouth to mouth
8. Hand to head
9. Hand to body
10. Mouth to body
11. Hand to genitals
12. Genitals to genitals

Rapport is established in the first three steps. Not being timid about moving on will yield further pleasures. For example, step number 6 (arm to waist) is often where all too many individuals stop, fearful of going for step 7, a kiss. But the Warlock should maintain and build on his rapport by placing his arm around the waist of his partner, then planting a kiss on her lips!

The key is the action itself, which shows confidence and intent – very sexy attributes of a man who knows what he wants. Practice creates more skill, but success comes from persistence and the willingness to fail.

SCENT – THE "SWEAT" SPOT

LaVey's astute observations on the Witch's power of scent in the practice of Lesser Magic shed light on the importance of exploiting numerous female olfactory essences in the mating game. He correctly observed that nature, in creating these magical odors (packed with pheromones) has already equipped both male and female with all the sexual stimulants they require. And research indeed supports the idea that smells are not only subliminal attraction signals but can be specifically exploited to create arousal. Women on average have 43 percent more cells in their olfactory bulbs than men, meaning a woman's sense of smell is much stronger than a man's. A good portion of her attraction is based on the subliminal messages her brain is receiving.

The Warlock's primary male scent (his hormone-heavy sweat) is his bestial beacon. LaVey wrote, "If you are a man, and wish to enchant a woman, allow the natural secretions of your body to pervade the atmosphere immediately around you, and work in animalistic contrast to the vestments of social politeness that you wear upon your back."

In 1995, Swiss biological researcher Claus Wedekind did a Major Histocompatibility Complex (MHC) test with a group of women (called "The Sweaty T-shirt experiment") to gauge how they'd react to male odors.

The study gathered 49 women and 44 men, selected for a variety of MHC gene types. The men wore a clean T-shirt for two nights. The shirts were then placed in seven different "sniff" boxes. Each girl was asked to smell the shirts and to describe each odor as to intensity, pleasantness, and sexiness. Most of the women reacted favorably to the smells, naturally preferring the scent of the male whose MHC gene was different from hers. The specific chemical makeup of the scent did two things: it triggered sexual arousal, but it also telegraphed that she was not related to him biologically, an efficient way to avoid the pitfalls of inbreeding.

Early in the 20th century, pioneering sexual researcher Havelock Ellis devoted 130 pages of his magnum opus on human sexuality, *Studies in the Psychology of Sex* to odors. He believed that although animal attraction is indeed preeminent, the sniffing has moved from the genitals to the upper body, further strengthening the argument that men's sweat – predominantly the armpits – is the center of scent and arousal. "It has thus happened that when personal odour acts as a sexual allurement it is in the armpit, in any case normally the chief focus of odour in the body, which mainly comes into play, together with the skin and hair," Ellis wrote.

In the latter part of the 20th century, male pheromones (androstenone) were being hawked as the "scent of Eros" that would magically open a girl's legs, particularly around ovulation. But old stale sweat (full of androstenone) is usually not attractive to women. The male sweat that attracts females is androstenol (produced when fresh male sweat is exposed to oxygen).

The trick is how to put the good odor to work as Lesser Magic seduction. The Warlock should not totally mask his armpit sweat with an overuse of deodorant, but instead wear loose-fitting shirts to allow oxidation. Some inorganic products like colognes and perfumes (the latter particularly for the Warlock seeking an androgynous appeal) have also been shown to appeal to females. The caveat is not to drown oneself so much that the smell is overpowering, but to instead apply just a hint of fragrance to suggest an exotic nature. This is one true example of "less is more." The slightest whiff of musk can make a man seem more masculine.

The type and ingredients in a fragrance are critical. A study at Ruhr-Universität Bochum in Germany suggests that the smell of roses can make women feel more romantic, while heliotropin (a chemical found in vanilla) has a comforting and sedative effect that may relax them.

Sandalwood, a key ingredient in many men's fragrances, is likened to androstenone, again emphasizing the sweat odor. Colognes with this ingredient could boost your appeal when blended with a hint of your armpit sweat. Colognes may also work because sex is not always the woman's endgame.

Presenting good (or bad) sweat brings a Warlock's personality to the fore, which is important to the female in casual social situations. But the Warlock is not wholly dependent on natural biological triggers, allowing all aspects of his true Self to shine and seduce, rather than just relying on his smell.

One Satanic Witch revealed, "I love the smell of a man's sweat, but usually only if I'm in the mood for sex. If I'm not in the mood and he's sweating all over me, it's a turn-off. The conditions have to be right for me to be seduced by his smell. When we're on a date or at a party I'd prefer he smell clean and fresh. The sex can always come later."

"Mood" is the operative word when it comes to how a Warlock should smell when attempting to seduce. In the throes of passion, some females have said that they can "release their inner slut" when their nose is in close contact with a man's penis, testicles, and anus, often taking deep breaths to amp up the lust. The biological combination of the secreting glands and the Law of the Forbidden often create a formidable and very exciting scenario.

SHARE EXCITEMENT TRANSFER

Excitation-transfer theory says that residual excitation from one stimulus will amplify the excitatory response to another stimulus. Simply stated, when you share an exhilarating or "safe" danger (eustress), that excitement (and resulting pleasure) is also experienced and remembered by your partner. Squeeze your partner's hand while a roller coaster plummets, and watch as the combination of thrill and protection form a powerful bond.

This is a valuable seduction technique as it leaves a lasting impression in your target's mind (and hopefully below the waist). The initial experience evokes a strong response to the danger, which is then calmed. For example, when watching a boxing match, a dirty fighter may spark anger in the spectator, but when he is later knocked out, the spectator experiences more pleasure because he or she is invested in the victory. This shared experience by two people creates the excitement-transfer bond – a very seductive tool.

HOW TO APPROACH A WOMAN – The Way of the Warlock

The strongest approach you can master when meeting a woman is to simply say "hello," followed by your name. A Warlock's state of mind – The Way of the Warlock – will exude his diabolical presence and be detected by the woman of his choice. Over-analyzing a situation is a mind killer and could lead to paralysis. Eliminate negative thoughts like *she's probably already got a boyfriend or I'll be humiliated if she rejects me.* When you initiate action, your Warlock Self naturally takes over.

Don't ever fear rejection, as only rejection and recovery will strengthen you. This especially holds true when you consider approaching a beautiful or accomplished woman you may feel is out of your league. Regardless of her wiles, pulchritude, or obvious assets, remember this if you are at all apprehensive: *Someone, somewhere is tired of fucking her.*

Once conversation starts, you will be close enough to see her eyes. Hypnotists and cold readers always check the subject's pupils – if they're dilated, the person is interested. This theory was confirmed by Dr. Eckhard Hess of the University of Chicago when he used it to formulate the science of pupillometrics. It has been around so long LaVey even mentioned it in *The Satanic Witch*.

Although the pupil dilation signal holds true in most cases, most men don't have the visual acuity to gauge this, in which case your gaze will undoubtedly be focused on pulchritude rather than pupils. But it's certainly worth a shot.

Eye movement – Visual Accessing Cues – is hotly disputed but may also determine a person's thinking, according to research done by NLP co-founders John Grinder, Frank Pucelik, and Richard Bandler. For example, each direction the eyes move – up, down, side to side – indicate a section of the brain that's recalling a sight, sound, or smell. Some say eyes moving to the left indicate lying. Concerning attraction, Warlocks should remember that a look downward usually indicates a submissive.

Satanists are masters of the art of the evil eye. Witches have always been known to fix a person's gaze to seduce and curse, but Warlocks need to develop the ability to lock the eyes and use their stare. Once your target's eyes lock for even a second, you've received the mating signal. Don't flinch or look away. Instead, drill into her eyes with a smoldering stare and a rakish smile (not a toothy grin!).

You must grasp and command the moment with your eyes. The method requires you to stare, occasionally looking away to avoid being comical or creepy. Look at the face about three quarters of the time, and at the eyes for between one and seven seconds. Any more and your target may feel uncomfortable. And NEVER direct your stare at a woman's breasts or other body parts.

The power of eye contact in seduction is a hotly researched subject. *Men's Health* magazine reported on a study at the University of Aberdeen, in which psychologist Claire Conway showed photos of men to hundreds of test subjects. Some of the men were casting sidelong glances at the camera (i.e. at the woman viewing the photo), while others looked straight into the lens. All the test subjects said that they found the men more attractive if they looked straight ahead – even if they looked angry or disgusted. The men who looked directly into the camera and smiled had the most success.

Raising eyebrows for as little as a tenth of a second also improves chances of a good impression, according to Kate Fox, a social psychologist at London's Social Issues Research Centre. Her "The SIRC Guide To Flirting" study states, "If you are desperate to attract the attention of an attractive stranger across a crowded party, you could try an eyebrow-flash.

"This makes your target think you must be a friend or acquaintance, even though he or she does not actually recognize you. When you approach, your target may already be wondering who you are. You can, if you are skillful, use this confusion to initiate a lively discussion about where you might have met before.

At a social gathering or party, first make eye contact, then follow up with your name. Avoid corny pick-up lines. If she's at all interested, your inner Warlock will present himself and she will gladly chat you up.

Another surefire method of attracting a woman's attention is to perform. Do a magic trick, play your guitar, recite a poem, even quote a book or movie. Do something that demonstrates your special, unique ability (whatever it may be), letting her know you're interesting while showcasing your confidence.

But beware; the wily Witch may use your vanity about your talent as a means to stroke your ego. Be realistic and don't let her flattery delude you. Know the limits of your talents, and know where to draw the line between genuine admiration and manipulation.

When advancing on your target, turn your awareness to your body's core. Feel your presence and ground your stance – then look into her eyes. Sense her emotions; be natural and spontaneous. Verbalize your genuine reactions, not canned lines. Listen with your body; don't think about it. Enjoy your environment. Use your hands to express yourself. Be humorous. Imagine life is pure pleasure, and as a Warlock you can always have your fill.

You must also show her how much she matters to you. She wants pleasure and you can provide what she needs. Women crave security for the long run but are intensely attracted to danger, the forbidden, risks, mystery (the lifeblood of seduction), and the appeal of darkness. You, as the embodiment of these traits, must play to those areas of her psyche.

See the world through her eyes. Act as if you are a slave to her charms (show your vulnerability, but keep it light and humorous). Think of yourself only as her provider of pleasure. Tell her you shun convention and that you believe strict morals are often forced and counterproductive.

As mentioned earlier, a common approach by PUAs is to "drop the NEG," that's basically a line that points out a woman's flaw in hopes that she will go out of her way to rectify that fault in your mind. It plays on her vanity and her insecurity – especially if she's in a group of other women.

The NEG was man's nasty recoil response to women feeling forced to "throw their weight around in relationships and the work world," as LaVey pointed out. Men may feel compelled to use derogatory language to throw women off guard (and let them stew on their shortcomings to create approval-seeking) or, to "level the playing field," showing the woman he's not just another feminized bland pussy. This approach can often be viewed as pure misogyny, but it should be understood that it's a product of social engineering and many men's lack of real confidence.

This tricky (and pretty shitty) method can work, especially with younger women or very self-centered and physically gorgeous women who have been praised and sought after all their lives. But the approach can backfire if the woman senses an antagonistic attitude. If you are comfortable using the NEG approach *never* deliberately insult a woman by pointing out obvious flaws or use hurtful words like "ugly," stupid," or "fat," even as a joke. It is not only ungentlemanly, but immediately demonstrates a weak, insecure male psyche. If you are inclined to use a NEG, make it subtle, like: "Are your eyes really that blue or are you wearing contact lenses?" If you are in a group and interested in a particularly talkative woman, ask: "Are you always this chatty?" And again, only try this approach with women under 25

· · · · · · · · · ◆ ◆ ◆ ◆ ◆ ◆ 🦄 ◆ ◆ ◆ ◆ ◆ ◆ · · · · · · · · ·

122

(and always prepare yourself to be immediately rejected as an abusive piece of crap).

As one Church of Satan Reverend who enjoys polyamory (more on this topic later) explains, "My most productive 'seductions' have been those in which the third step was 'Expression of Desire.' I do not use pickup lines or gimmicks. I simply, clearly, and honestly state my interest. Usually something like, 'As I get to know you I am really interested in spending more time with you. I find you attractive and interesting. If you would be open to getting dinner or going dancing or hitting some concerts or parties together, I would really like that.' And then I shut up and let her speak. I apply no pressure. If she demurs in any way, I just leave it that I am interested and available. Lots of open and honest communication is critical, particularly about level of interest, the kinds of activities I would like to do with her, my own relationship and availability status, and the like. I never lie or even vaguely misrepresent for sex or seduction. All cards are played face up on the table."

BE THE "HERO" – EMPLOY THE SEDUCTION OF SURRENDER

The consummate Warlock seducer's goal is to be his intended's ultimate hero. Childhood fantasies of Prince Charming and the noble Black Knight make a woman long for a man who listens to her, understands her, and makes her feel as if she is everything. But she also dreams of Casanova and Don Juan. Despite an outward air of strength or confidence, a woman wants to surrender her problems, desires, body, and soul to a man who in turn will be her true hero.

This personification need not be confused with the typical definition of hero (firefighter, cop, soldier) but rather the Warlock who can whisk a woman away from a particular problem, circumstance, or boring life struggle, and still be soft when needed. He must first listen without immediately trying to "fix" the situation, as men are naturally inclined to do. By all means be excruciatingly attentive, but don't be her therapist. Listening to the problems that aren't specific to you as a couple may make her associate you with her unhappiness. The line between "I'm your knight in shining armor" and "I'm your doormat" is admittedly fine (and often subject to change at a moment's notice).

Warlocks are particularly suited to becoming ideal "hero seducers." The Warlock who wants to play the hero must use his naturally dark leanings but temper them with the promise of vulnerability to the right woman. He will surrender his strength and safety for his intended! A woman will surrender her body, mind, and true love to the sincerity he shows.

Witness the recent proliferation of "Bigfoot erotica" that features a monstrous creature aggressively taking a woman. The surrender is fictional of course, but it illustrates the fantasy desire to be ravaged by a massively powerful creature (with clear social and physical issues) first dominating but then showing a surprising vulnerability. Think "Beauty and the Beast." The brute strength is there, but it is surrendered to her love, whereby the Beast becomes the hero.

The Warlock who masters the use of his dark, Satanic Self to bring out his beastly "hero seducer" will win any woman he chooses.

EMBRACE YOUR BAD REPUTATION – BE THE SCOUNDREL

But what if you're not a hero? What if you're a scoundrel?

While the above is certainly true, many women look for a different hero entirely. The Warlock who has genuinely earned a bad reputation in love affairs, trysts, and relationships should embrace his Devilish pedigree instead of denying it or making excuses. After all, the Warlock persona is about mystery – dark and dangerous. That bad boy appeal – the scoundrel – is intoxicating to women and is a proven aphrodisiac.

Any need to whitewash that image is obviously contradictory to this Warlock, so why not exploit it? Remember, in seduction, the Warlock needs to be *desired*, not *liked!* The Law of the Forbidden is a powerful ally.

The caveat of course is *don't take this too far!* If you are deliberately hurtful and inconsiderate, your scoundrel persona will shift from saucy to shitty, people will see you for the self-centered asshole you truly are, and interest in you will wither away.

Successful scoundrels juggle extramarital affairs and trysts by becoming the consummate liar. You must have an exceptional memory and be an extraordinary strategist to make sure you always cover your tracks. This is dangerous ground, but if you choose to play here, be prepared to have your story ready and your lies in order – or suffer the consequences!

Lady Caroline Lamb, a lover of Lord Byron, described the romantic poet as "mad, bad, and dangerous to know."

RELEASE YOUR BEAST

Above all, do the man's job, which is take the lovemaking to her. Release the woman in her. Tell her your desires, what you want and what you want her to do. Release your beast! Many women long to be taken (but not coerced or forced in a rape scenario). They want to be aggressively consumed by their lover. Use your Satanic strength to initiate and orchestrate the dance. You can take turns taking the lead later, but you must be the first to initiate the act. Women really do want you to impress them, because they use sex as a release into their fantasy lives.

BEDROOM ETIQUETTE

The under-reported truth: Many men are lousy in bed. Just eavesdrop on two or more women having lunch. Most men are in a rush to have their own orgasm (and some just pop too easily) without any consideration for the proper foreplay required to perform as an ideal lover. Foreplay is such a misnomer! Teasing, touching, stroking, whispering. That's where the real magic builds. All your tools of seduction lay the groundwork, but when the rubber hits the road, all the fantasies and promises you used to seduce your woman must now culminate in skillful, proper lovemaking.

Foreplay begins the moment a couple is together, not the moment they get into bed! Use everything in lovemaking – gazes, touches, eye contact, and NLP techniques. Of course there are no solid "rights and wrongs," but a slow and giving approach allows seduction to simmer to a boil. Pay close attention to how she reacts.

Myriad self-help resources can be tapped by the curious Warlock, but the best approach is still trial and error. It sounds obvious, but there is no "one size fits all," and every woman's needs are different. Your "signature move" clitoris lick may send one woman to the moon and another to the 7-Eleven to rent a movie.

Approach your lovemaking as you approach your life – be confident but *listen and feel* your woman's responses and act accordingly. Ask questions (dirty talk helps), and gauge her body's movements, breaths, and sounds. You will quickly learn what pleases her if you just pay attention. Try body massages that include stroking (and pulling!) her hair, rubbing her neck, shoulders, back, and ass, all the while whispering how hot she makes you. Hearing your passion will fuel her desire.

Sexologist Dr. Ava Cadell of Loveology University suggests a few more techniques. For example, while undoing her bra, kiss, nibble and lick all over her breasts. Put her nipple in your mouth and roll your tongue around the perimeter. Try placing an ice cube in your mouth, lick the nipple, then do it again without the cube. The alternating warm/cold sensation is highly erotic.

As the gentleman Warlock, make it your duty to let *her achieve orgasm first* (or with you simultaneously) whenever possible. This will immediately set you apart from the others. If you orgasm first, be sure to help her get hers immediately after. Also keep in mind that orgasm is not always the goal, especially for women. Often times the sexual experience itself suffices. Remember, a woman's passion is circular, not linear.

DOES SIZE MATTER?

Penis size, despite what any man will tell you, matters a lot less than you think, so let's finally put the size myth to rest. Most women really don't care unless it is astonishingly small (less than two inches) or extremely huge (you want me to put that *Where?!*).

The good news is... you're normal. *Men's Health* magazine reports a best possible average of 3.6 inches flaccid and 5.2 inches hard for 90% of the population. Research from BJU International, a respected urological medical journal that studied more than 15,000 data points from men ranging in age from 17-91, found only about 2% of men were abnormally small or large, despite the angst felt in every high school shower in the world.

POSITION TIPS TO ACCENTUATE SIZE

Not only can it get a bit dull, the missionary position isn't much of a showcase for the average penis. Here are two methods to take advantage of every inch you have to offer.

First, lay her on her stomach, raising her pelvic area with a pillow. Enter her from behind with your weight supported on your arms. This creates a tighter fit, making you feel larger inside her.

The second method is the popular girl-on-top or "cowgirl" – a staple of porn films. You lie on your back with the lady straddling you. This is good for deep insertion and lets her get every inch of you. It also puts her in complete control of the thrusting. The "reverse cowgirl" is exactly as it sounds; this way she's facing away (riding with her back to you).

The mechanics of sex are of course vital to a successful seduction, and must be tailored to the individual woman (or women) in your bed. We asked some prominent Witches about sexual prowess:

– Sex is vitally important, but not something you have to stress over. Obviously, you won't be very functional if you do. It is such a personal thing that the woman you're with will hopefully voice her likes and dislikes so you can navigate those waters together. Just relax into it and see what works for both of you.

– The last thing any woman wants is to feel like you're running your playbook of moves on her, the same way you've done it with every other woman you nailed. We don't want to be the latest notch on your bedpost, but we also don't want to think you just got a new manual on killer sex moves and we're your guinea pig. Ideally, it should be a shared exploration, even if it's just one night. Look at her, smell her, feel her living flesh and envelop yourself in who she is, what she wants – not just in bed, but in the core of her being… Or at least do a convincing job of faking it. It really is true that if you can stay up until two in the morning pretending to be interested in what she has to say, you'll reach your goal. Of course, in a perfect world, it would be a lot more fun if you found a woman you actually

respect and don't have to fake it with. But that doesn't always happen for women either. So, depending on your goals, you can both fake your way through a fairly decent night (or month or year) of ecstasy, if that's the aim. Or you can both have a fulfilling short-term relationship and possibly broaden your techniques and your understanding of females if you risk a bit of yourself and actually show up.

— That's something that can be taught/learned. It's nice to be around someone who is not a complete novice, but a Warlock should be completely aware of his own body. That really is the key.

— A man needs to know what he's doing and be confident in the bedroom (or whatever room).

— I'm old enough that I don't need to have sex every day, but when I do want it, I damn well want it to be spectacular. He'd better bring his A Game, because I certainly bring mine.

— Skill is important because sex differentiates an intimate relationship from a platonic relationship. You must be on the same page.

THE POWER AND PITFALLS OF PORN

Pornography has never been more explicit or available, offering a true Disneyland of decadence for everyone. And to the delight of many Satanists, the availability of such a new and varied smorgasbord of smut has opened up a number of lustful treats for the senses (and experiments in the bedroom). Harnessing its ability to create lustful fantasies is indeed Lesser Magic and a powerful tool for satisfaction, especially when those scenarios can be played out with a willing partner!

New wave porn has also allowed Warlocks to "expose" their partners to sex acts they've always fantasized about but didn't have the guts to discuss. The intense visual stimulation of porn has given Satanists even more fuel for their dirty minds. New techniques can be discovered and explored using porn as a guidebook.

But remember: Most porn scenarios are scripted. Take it from someone who has been intimate with the adult industry for more than 20 years – your girlfriend or wife is not a porn actress, so don't expect to play out the same scenarios unless you both agree ahead of time. Porn stars are in it for the money and are absolutely acting for the viewer. A number I've known who have relationships outside of porn get their sexual kicks from pretty normal stuff, not sucking three cocks at once or seeing how many kitchen tools can be shoved into their gaping asses. Fulfill your desires, but know the line between fantasy and reality. Choking may work in a fetish video, but it's usually disastrous in the bedroom.

Of course there are exceptions, and Satanists are typically freer about their carnal passions, but expecting to duplicate the extremes in commercial porn will lead to frustration. The wise Warlock will use porn to his advantage. Embrace the fantasies and expose them to your partner. If she bites, then you've hit the mark! If not, use your own fantasy and ECI to heighten the experience.

THE ANTIDOTE TO THE "POWER OF THE PUSSY"

In circumstances where Warlocks find themselves at the mercy of their desires, there is an antidote. Witches (and women in general) do indeed hold a mesmerizing, often awesome power over men that can lead to debilitating frustration. Let's face it: We sometimes find ourselves slaves to their magic, worshiping at the altar of pulchritude, despite our better judgment.

Fortunately, the remedy is the simple idea of *patience*. The moment a woman catches a Warlock's eye, she knows his desire and lust are rising. She can sense his interest and will begin to use her abilities to flirt and create excitement – often regardless of whether she is seriously interested or not. If she is interested, she'll go all in and use her trusted methods to stroke the man's ego (always the key to a woman's seduction). Once in her grasp, the game begins, the Warlock proceeds to the next steps, and sometimes ends up in her bed.

When a woman initially shows interest but interrupts the process, she is either weighing her options, hasn't fully made up her mind, or is simply playing hard to get. If the Warlock is sincerely interested he must use all of his seduction techniques. He must turn the tables and picture himself as the "prize," employ his "cat and string" techniques, then sit back and wait. If there's no response from a woman after initial interest, the Warlock's strength and patience must take command. If there's genuine interest on her part, she will make a move. It may take days, weeks, or even months, but if she wants him, she will wonder why the Warlock hasn't pursued her and she will take action.

If too much time passes, the mood is lost and the Warlock must chalk it up to experience and forget her. Move on and "spin a new plate." The initial chemistry, one-night stand, or whatever early attraction there was simply wasn't enough. And sorry to say dear fellows, if this is the case, you didn't have her anyway, so why waste more time worrying about her?

Of course, women don't always articulate in words or actions what they really want – biology, genetics, and subconscious impulses often run the show – but time usually tells. And know this: You cannot control someone's feelings; only your reactions. Although there may be some masochistic pleasure in rejection, take it for what it's worth – a learning experience. Prolonged agony steals precious hours of life that could be focused on pleasure, so quit moping and move on!

SEDUCTION AND THE SATANIC WITCH

Although the general rules of seduction apply to all women, the Warlock must first recognize the power of the Satanic Witch. She is his sister in Satanism and an expert at using her wiles to woo and work her man.

Our Witches are savvier about the game of seduction because they've fine-tuned their craft. A Satanic Witch knows a Warlock will be aware of (and anticipate) her enchanting capabilities. She will take this as a challenge and step up her game. She'll initially appeal to the Warlock's core Minority Self whatever that may be (if you've not read *The Satanic Witch*, now is the time!) and satisfy those needs deep within – usually meaning a particular fetish – so watch out!

Her bewitching abilities aren't an insurmountable barrier for the Warlock – the challenge is just tougher because the playing field is more level. The good news is that because they share the Satanic philosophy (and a diabolical outlook on the world), the game will mostly be deciding who plays the seducer and who plays the *seducee*. If a long-term relationship is the goal, we hope the dance will be deliciously in sync and everyone gets what he or she wants. Life is indeed a give-and-take proposition and when it's Witch vs. Warlock, the desired outcome should always be mutual indulgence and satisfaction. If it isn't, the Warlock must re-evaluate his target's desires. If it's totally physical and never passes the mutual tease phase, he must bow out or attempt to fix the situation. If the Warlock isn't igniting the fire in her mind, even if he is her match on the LaVey Personality Synthesizer, he will not last long in her bed.

A WORD ABOUT HEARTBREAK

It is worth noting that in the event seduction does indeed turn to love, there is a good chance you will have your heart broken. And as already mentioned, despite a Warlock's steely demeanor, things go awry and the male animal simply does not take heartbreak as well as the female. This is probably a combination of bruised ego, the drop in sex-generated hormones, or the indignity of a loss to a competitor.

Not to belabor what has been sung in torch songs for decades, suffice it to say that when an affair is done, it's done. You'll know it in your gut despite your yearnings for reconciliation. Apply the three-time rule and move on after three failed attempts. It applies to reconciliation as well as pursuit. You cannot control the affections of others. If she had real love she may even come back to you... but don't count on it.

The best a Warlock can do is to embrace his pain (never deny it – it is part of the healing process) and remember he was attractive and appealing enough to make that person fall in love with him. Use the pain of breakups – all of them – to remind you of your inner strength and the glory of this, your one and only life. Whatever changed (if you didn't change yourself) was most likely out of your control. Take prior victories as positives in your life – a bona fide confidence builder – and keep them in your mind as major accomplishments and achievements in seduction! We all lose at some point – the secret is to view the loss not as a failure, but as a learning experience – ammunition for the next, more deserving conquest!

And remember, NOTHING is as bad as it seems when it comes to losing love. You will get over it and you will love again. And the fastest way to get *over* someone is to get *under* someone new! Don't waste too much time pining. As Sinatra sang, "Torches should be drowned in champagne."

HOW TO END A RELATIONSHIP

If a relationship goes bad (and they do), and you feel you must extricate yourself, a Warlock above all needs to be a gentleman. Gently but firmly say you've lost romantic feelings. Don't use trite clichés like "it's not you, it's me." Women instinctively know when things are bad, so man up and tell her that you're both headed for disaster if this bad match continues. Don't tell her there's someone else (even if there is), don't point out faults, don't say you've tried. Just say it's not working and you need to move on. Her hurt will wane over time and you walk away knowing you acted with integrity.

Above all, DO NOT BREAK UP BY EMAIL, TEXT or some other pathetic digital smokescreen, even if it's what everyone else in your social circle does. This is a cowardly move and it will brand you as such among your acquaintances (and more importantly with any woman who gets wind of it).

A WORD ABOUT POLYAMORY

The relationship dynamic of polyamory is a 21st century, modernized successor to the open marriage movement of the 1970s. Sometimes called "non-monogamy," partners have consensual sex and intimate relationships involving more than two people, with the knowledge and approval of everyone involved. The movement has gained momentum in the past 10 years, and dozens of books on the topic are available.

It's an interesting and obviously attractive lifestyle for Warlocks seeking to "have their cake and eat it too," and also for women to add more players to this newly expanded field of sex and romance (something many Satanic Witches have been enjoying all along). The idea falls in line nicely with Satanism's all-accepting carnal philosophy. The caveat, of course, is that human nature is still in play, and no matter what lengths the parties go to to avoid it, feelings are often deeply hurt.

It should also be noted that polyamory seems best suited for those in the age range 20-40, because they have not been so overwhelmingly conditioned to traditional coupling. Whether polyamory can work for most people is hotly debated, especially for older generations. Even some younger folks struggle with the triangulating trysts. As mentioned earlier, the 2015 *Vanity Fair* article on Tinder reported that most girls still want just one boyfriend and/or husband to keep the cave safe at night.

One Warlock in a polyamorous relationship revealed that he indeed struggled with "sharing" the woman that he'd grown to love. The remedy he said is a continued and open line of communication.

Magister Robert Merciless has been enjoying this lifestyle for years. He finds polyamory particularly compatible with Satanism and its high valuation of sexual fulfillment as well as "responsibility to the responsible" and the rejection of herd conformity. Satanists view the human species as just another animal, living a carnal life consistent with natural instincts barely suppressed by socialization. So, for many Satanists, non-monogamy is more natural.

Merciless describes polyamory as a "a world of many loves" and describes a lifestyle characterized by open, honest, intimate, loving relationships with more than one person. The lifestyle is distinct from "cheating" in that all partners are aware of all other partners and relationships are openly disclosed to all parties.

"The Satanic Warlock who pursues this lifestyle should be quite masterful at the tools of Lesser Magic, including careful attention to the emotions of others, good timing, and clear, sensitive and well-considered communication. Anything less than open, honest dialogue and negotiation will make these relationships rocky. In contrast, however, a Satanic Warlock knows that almost anything can be negotiated. In that vein, properly managed and cared for, open or polyamorous relationships are a source of great satisfaction, fulfillment, and joy," Merciless says.

Readers interested in knowing more can read *The Ethical Slut* by Dossie Easton, *Opening Up* by Tristan Taormino, *More Than Two* by Franklin Veaux, and *Sex at Dawn* by Christopher Ryan.

A WORD ABOUT INFIDELITY

A word of caution regarding infidelity, aka cheating. If a woman is cheating on her partner or spouse (anything from sharing fantasies, sexy texts and secret emails to actually having sex), it's a safe bet she is unhappy with some aspect of her relationship. Her motives may vary – looking for a "shoehorn lover" to pry her out of her relationship, seeking a temporary distraction, or feeling neglected or bored. Whatever it is, it's *something*. Most women will not entertain an affair if their primary relationship is strong.

If you think you're immune to this and knowingly engage in an affair with someone else's partner or mate, keep in mind that if she cheated with you, there's a good chance she will cheat on you!

And despite Satanists' abhorrence of guilt, infidelity is a slippery slope and ALWAYS a double-edged sword. Unless both parties are moving in the same direction, the affair is likely to blow up. In the event you get caught red-handed, the best advice is like the old joke says: never admit to anything, even if you're caught in her bedroom with your pants around your ankles. Buy time while you turn the disaster into a joke. Lie! Lie! Lie! *It's not what it looks like. That was an unfortunate wardrobe malfunction. Wait – this ISN'T my bedroom?* Say what you need to and run like hell. This is the time to do your "Father of Lies" act – for your own damn good! To confront an irate spouse or boyfriend is not only stupid but also dangerous. If her spouse gets huffy or threatening, don't *defend* your actions; *attack*. Point out that your bedmate seduced you. If she has no respect for her vows, why should *you*? Then run!

If you still prefer to shop in another man's closet (and you're not progressive enough to try polyamory or less dangerous affairs), take those pleasures for what they're worth, while they last, but expect it to end badly. In the off chance both partners leave their mates to form a new couple, by all means enjoy!

THERE ARE NO LONG-DISTANCE RELATIONSHIPS

Regardless of what you've seen or heard, there's no such thing as a long-distance relationship. Even in the best circumstances, where two people are deep in limerence, the strain of loneliness, doubt, fear, and lustful within-reach temptations eventually win out.

Warlocks who prefer to keep women at a distance are better advised to use the "ship in every port" tactic and establish a stable of women to enjoy whenever and wherever they go.

THE OVER-40 WARLOCK

Although basic Satanic seduction methods can be applied by the over-40 Warlock, he faces challenges from aging, hormone loss (testosterone decreases 1 percent a year starting at age 30), porn over-saturation (yes, it's a thing), and even overwork. In other words… shit just wears out.

Most men over 40 will experience some form of erectile dysfunction (ED) or a loss of sex drive. The reasons vary depending on the individual, but it's usually the result of the physical and hormonal connections between brain and penis not being as strong as when a man is young. That's the bad news.

The good news is that sex can still be enjoyed regularly and with many partners well into the 80s and 90s.

Once again, it's about confidence and self-assuredness. Character built on Satanic principles creates a palpable attribute that women notice. Playing the worldly Warlock card can work wonders for those who worry they're losing their male edge, easing the graying Warlock into a new phase of life. Whether he's 40, 50, 60, 70, or beyond, knowing the

Warlock Self improves with age regardless of physical ability will fortify his confidence. I know Warlocks who have taken pleasure with 20- and 30-year-old women well into their 60's. Women who say dashing older men get away with murder because of their "distinguished" looks are absolutely right!

Concerning ED, many such occurrences are more mental than physical (trying too hard to regain a one-time lost erection spirals into a vicious mental cycle). The penis is a remarkable organ, dependent on a number of physical and mental processes. Depression, drugs and alcohol and prescription drug interactions (blood pressure medication in particular) all contribute to ED. One or more of these in play and you might as well get a couple of popsicle sticks and a rubber band. At this point tactile stimulation becomes more important for an erection than fantasy.

Still, the harder one tries, the less he succeeds. I have heard many stories of over-40 Warlocks who found themselves in bed with beautiful desirable women and just couldn't perform. It's more common than most men want to believe or admit. But it absolutely doesn't have to be a permanent condition.

If a doctor rules out physical problems, drugs like Viagra and Cialis may be all the Warlock needs. They work by increasing blood flow to the penis and have been FDA approved for years. The drugs serve two purposes: first, they *make* an erection happen. Then, once the Warlock sees he is physically capable, the cycle of frustration is broken. The long-term goal is to simply relax, knowing that thinking too hard isn't helping. If he can't perform this time, he will next time. Better to make this all about the woman's body, her softness, smell, eyes, and the pleasure she's receiving rather than fixate on a temporary situation. She won't mind.

The truth is the male animal is biologically and anthropologically suited to have sex (however he defines it) until he dies. Hail Satan!

APRHODISIACS and LIBIDO BOOSTERS

If the sight of a well-turned ankle, ample rear, or perky breasts isn't enough to fire your carnal crank, you've probably looked into libido enhancing solutions like supplements and drugs. The good news is that real improvement can come from regular exercise, eating organic food, and having regular sex – it really can be that simple! Supplements help some men, but it's debatable whether the results come from the supplement itself or the placebo effect. Again, much depends on a man's physical condition and psychological state.

Performance anxiety is often the culprit. Keep in mind that no man bats 1,000 – we are complicated machines that sometimes break down. If you are agreeable to using drugs or supplements, by all means do. If you choose this route, you have a few options beyond just Viagra and Cialis.

Supplements and herbs promise to boost libido and performance. These products are designed either to help the blood flow to the penis (like L-Arginine), or boost a sagging libido (like Horny Goat Weed).

Try any or all of these, but know there are no miracles. Be warned before you plunk down $50 a month for some super sex igniter – most are a scam and work minimally if at all. Many are actually dangerous. Testosterone levels play an enormous part in a man's desire and thus his performance. As we age, this amazing hormone diminishes. And although there are many "testosterone booster" products on the market, they must be used with caution and under a doctor's care. These products should only be used by men whose blood tests indicate very low levels of testosterone. Men who are not clinically deficient can experience troubling side effects like acne and breast enlargement.

Aphrodisiacs are also hit or miss, but can help in lowering inhibitions. The staples (oysters and chocolate) may work, but in reality they're probably more psychological than physical stimulants. Liquor might seem quicker but will shut the whole thing down if you over-imbibe. Some cigars have also been known to "buzz the libido."

A simple but often overlooked libido booster is just having more orgasms, with a partner or alone. "Use it or lose it" as they say. Orgasms help keep your prostate gland healthy and also boost hormone production to keep the horny part of your brain online.

LIBIDO AND PERFORMANCE BOOSTING SUPPLEMENTS

L-Arginine (performance)

Horny Goat Weed

Maca Root

Polypodium Vulgare (libido and performance)

Yohimbe (performance – caution, can elevate heart rate)

Ginko Biloba (libido and performance)

Korean Ginseng

Muira Puama

Katana

Damiana (libido and performance)

VigRX Oil (brand name)

Fenugreek

Pomegranate Juice

APHRODISIACS

Oysters

Chocolate

Truffles

Clove

Patchouli

Musk Oil

Okra

Sandalwood

Gypsyweed Rose Petals

THE SATANIC MASCULINITY METER

Be it known – NO man is completely masculine, despite considering himself to be the manliest or most macho of men. The very term "masculinity" may describe someone who exhibits strength, confidence, bravery, general attractiveness, and sexual virility, but it is a broad term and makes no specifications as to type.

Where the Satanic Warlock is concerned, masculinity indeed takes many forms. Satanism gives us a leg up, but there is also a swing element

The Satanic Masculinity Meter

If the Warlock is:

He can date:

If the Warlock is:		He can date:
HANDSOME, RICH* AND FAMOUS	10	STUNNING MODEL TYPES
RICH AND FAMOUS	9	SOME MODELS/ACTRESSES
VERY HANDSOME	8	VERY ATTRACTIVE/ SOME SUCCESSFUL WOMEN
RICH/ATTRACTIVE**	7	
RICH	6	MOST ATTRACTIVE/ SOME ABOVE AVERAGE WOMEN
ATTRACTIVE	5	SOME ATTRACTIVE/ SUCCESSFUL WOMEN
AVERAGE/ BELOW AVERAGE/ SUCCESSFUL	4	SOME ATTRACTIVE/ MOST AVERAGE WOMEN
	3	SOME AVERAGE/MOST BELOW ATTRACTIVE
BELOW AVERAGE	2	BELOW AVERAGE ATTRACTIVE WOMEN
FLAWED	1	DESPERATE/SOME BELOW AVERAGE ATTRACTIVE WOMEN

* INDICATES MONETARY AND PERSONAL SUCCESS IN CHOSEN FIELD
** ATTRACTIVE CAN DENOTE INTELLIGENCE, WIT AND SUCCESS IN ADDITION TO LOOKS

(including career and wealth) that influences how we perceive masculinity.

But as we saw in the Archetype descriptions, masculinity can mean almost anything and be applied across all character types. In the mating game, the "more" masculinity a man has, the more likely he will be successful in finding and bedding a mate. In other words, we need a reality check to determine the type of woman we can attract and have a relationship with so we can avoid frustration, unwanted angst, and whining about "why that girl doesn't like me."

The Satanic Masculinity Meter is a simple 1-to-10 scale, with the highest level of masculine traits and accomplishments being at level 10 and the lowest at 1.

A rich, young, classically handsome celebrity will easily be a 10 and score a 10-level woman (his corresponding ideal): no surprises there. Conversely, an unattractive working stiff who won't even try will drag his ass in at 1, giving him zero hope of scoring with any woman of discernment. Most men fall somewhere in between, but an honest assessment can be a real eye-opener. Your "score" lets you know where you stand now and what work needs to be done to get the level of mate you desire.

You may notice the test is more than a little rigged: Money and fame/power guarantee even the most repulsive man gets the 10 slot. Unfair but true, and for this exercise you must see what IS, not what you want to see. The Meter is not designed to discourage a Warlock from pursuing any woman he really wants. It is an indicator, showing his real strengths and weaknesses.

Still, this idea is difficult to get across without insulting both genders. Obviously, a 10 Warlock can score a Victoria's Secret model or the female head of surgery at a renowned hospital, while a 1 or 2 may have to settle for someone far less glamorous and accomplished. This isn't about being mean; it's about being realistic. Fortunately for men, looks, power, wealth and style can often be trumped by intelligence, humor and warmth. Women aren't machines. Lucky for us, most of them judge men on a lot more than just money.

Age is another big consideration. Unfortunately, the older a Warlock is, the less likely he is to score with the young and beautiful unless he is indeed rich, and/or famous, no matter where he falls on the Meter.

The Meter serves the Warlock as a general barometer of what he's up against, helping him avoid many hours of frustration. Many women without modern good looks will be dismissed by the short-sighted 10s, only to prove themselves diamonds in the rough (and spitfires in the sack) for the lower-numbered men who are smart enough to choose them.

THE INFLUENCE OF FILM

I was 10 years old, pre-pubescent but still aware of something very different and exciting about the ladies. Mom's friends, women at department store make-up counters, my music teacher – they all had something I knew I wanted but just couldn't put my finger on (or in?).

My epiphany hit full swing when my mom took me to see "The Nutty Professor," starring Jerry Lewis. Jerry played a bumbling nerd scientist with buckteeth, glasses, and wild hair. Far from "cool" by prevailing 1960s standards.

But Jerry's character soon transformed (à la Jekyll & Hyde… or a *werewolf*) into Buddy Love – a smooth-talking, cigarette-smoking, powder-blue-jacket-wearing ladies man and seducer! This was my moment of enlightenment. I knew I could be anyone I wanted to be (in true Satanic fashion).

So many movies taught me so much about the way of the seducer. I pored over every film, studying those Lotharios to absorb their methods and style. In fact, kissing a young girl's hand for the first time (imitating Errol Flynn in "The Adventures of Don Juan") got me access to the rest of her physical delights. Magic! So much to learn from these fictional lady-killers, I reasoned, and now I share some of these classic movies with you. Each has its own brand of Devilish charm – some stealthy, some sweet, and some just funny. Study them and their de facto Satanist protagonists.

"9 1/2 Weeks" (Mickey Rourke)
"Alfie" (Michael Caine)
"American Gigolo" (Richard Gere)

"Angel Heart" (Robert DeNiro)

"Boomerang" (Eddie Murphy)

"Casanova 70" (Marcello Mastroianni)

"Crazy Stupid Love" (Ryan Gosling)

"Cruel Intentions" (Ryan Phillippe)

"Dangerous Liaisons" (John Malkovich)

"Don Juan DeMarco" (Johnny Depp)

"Dracula" (Frank Langella)

"Eyes Wide Shut" (Tom Cruise)

"Fifty Shades of Grey" (Jamie Dornan)

"Giacomo Casanova" (Heath Ledger)

"Gone With the Wind" (Clark Gable)

James Bond Films (Pick one; they all work!)

"La Dolce Vita" (Marcello Mastroianni)

"Magnolia" (Tom Cruise)

"Meet Joe Black" (Brad Pitt)

"Moonstruck" (Nicolas Cage)

"Shampoo" (Warren Beatty)

"The Adventures of Don Juan" (Errol Flynn)

"The Devils" (Oliver Reed)

"The Devil's Advocate" (Al Pacino)

"The Libertine" (Johnny Depp)

"The Man Who Loved Women" (original Francis Truffaut version, funeral scene)

"The Seducer" (Jon Ferguson)

"The Tender Trap" (Frank Sinatra)

"The Witches of Eastwick" (Jack Nicholson)

"Three in the Attic" (Christopher Jones)

"Tom Jones" (Albert Finney)

"What Women Want" (Mel Gibson)

warlock wisdom

- Seduction happens in a woman's mind.
- A Warlock's physical appearance is secondary to his overall persona.
- Looks matter but are not always deal breakers.
- Men are the romantics, not women.
- Use pleasure as a weapon.
- Neither a "nice guy," nor an asshole be.
- Embrace and use your dark image to seduce.
- Be mysterious and unpredictable.
- Be unique and flaunt it. If you're not, add something that makes you unique.
- Appeal to a woman's "feral urge" by finding and exploiting her secret triggers.
- Beautiful women are tired of hearing they're beautiful. Seduce her mind.
- Show women undivided attention. Be obsessive over details.
- Do things impulsively with your intended in mind. Surprise with small, unusual gifts.
- Use the push/pull technique. Tease, and then withdraw.
- Never beg – unless you've screwed up.
- Never ask if you're "liked"/"loved."
- Never verbalize your faults and weaknesses.
- Use your intended's "boomerang words."
- Shower your intended with her ECI vanity/ego triggers (music, movies, books, art).

more

warlock wisdom

- Attend special events with your lover to attach yourself to those memories.

- Remember details and important dates.

- Don't rest on your "good looks." (If you haven't been told you're good-looking or beautiful more than 500 times in your lifetime, you're ordinary.)

- The old saying "someone's probably sick of fucking her" is true regardless of a woman's physical attractiveness.

- Identify and fill the void in her life.

- Don't appear needy, ever – be patient in all matters of the heart. The antidote to the "Power of the Pussy" is patience.

- Devote yourself to pleasure. Disdain convention.

- Be her hero and her scoundrel.

- There is no "one" person for you. We have many potential mates. Do not dwell on a loss.

- Know that a broken heart isn't the end of the world. It will pass. You've accomplished/seduced/won that love that is ending. You will again.

- The fastest way to get over someone is to get on someone new.

- Embrace your bad reputation. The Warlock's goal is to be "desired, not liked."

- Get creative to escape from dangerous romantic entanglements.

CHAPTER SEVEN

SEX MAGIC – THE WARLOCK AS SEX MAGICIAN

**"Make only the engagement, and at once
All will be pleasure – I have rare devices
And my craft will show thee many marvels
Right strange and merry scenes will conjure up;
Sights shalt thou see that man hath never seen."
MEPHISTOPHELES, Goethe's *Faust***

For centuries, occult lore has been hyping the mystical powers of Sex Magic, including Tantra, famous for marathon sessions in which the man often forgoes orgasm to create a more cosmic level of pleasure. While Satanic Sex Magic sometimes involves postponing orgasm to build intensity, we don't go to nearly this extreme. A host of other treatises catalog tricks for delivering intense orgasms or conjuring a sultry succubus to pleasure you in your dreams. But Warlocks need only concern themselves with the true Satanic goal: an indulgent, mind-blowing, real-world orgasm, either on its own or as part of a Greater Magic lust ritual to manifest material gain or the ideal sex partner.

Satanists shun "sacred sexuality," dismissing it as occultnik malarkey, with its kooky menstrual blood and semen alchemy, necrophilia, and other silly blasphemies. Some traditions, particularly the Hindus, rely heavily on these so-called potent elixirs to boost the libido during sex. Order Templi Orientis's founder Aleister Crowley borrowed from them to concoct his own "magickal elixir of life" from male and female sexual fluids. He named his creation *Elixir Rubeus* and called it "El Rub." Several entries in Crowley's magical diaries mention "the effluvium of Babalon, the Scarlet Woman, which is the menstruum of the lunar current."

Hilariously, accounts from the Great Beast 666's O.T.O. associates indicated that the concoction never actually worked… until he mixed it with alcohol – a complete shock (to no one).

Other Sex Magic luminaries include Paschal Beverly Randolph, Ida Craddock, Russian mystics Maria de Naglowska, Rasputin (better-known for his erotic spell casting and sexual prowess than his magical workings), and Magistra Waytz's own distant relative G.I. Gurdjieff. Others contributed to the practice but their workings were basically designed to titillate more than conjure up any real demons or worldly treats. Paschal Beverly Randolph, the famed Rosicrucian, actually believed sexual energy could change the world and was the greatest force in Nature. One thing we can agree on!

Intricate Eastern Buddhism and Taoism sex rituals and so-called Black Mass rites (famously touted for being performed in the nude) abound in occult literature and legend. Those interested in studying esoteric Sex Magic will find everything from sensory deprivation and bondage to Western ceremonial magical systems in Paganism and Chaos Magic.

But Satanism celebrates pure carnality, which means we are driven by the pleasures of the flesh. We're not interested in laughable left-hand wizards, waving their dicks like magic wands in hopes of piercing the hymen of a demoness, becoming an ersatz deity, or birthing a separate sexual entity from a couple's orgasmic energy. Sure it's fun to ritualize, and we humans need that. But better to leave the really wacky stuff to the professionals like Thelemite occultist Jack Parsons. In 1945 he teamed up with Scientology founder L. Ron Hubbard to conduct the O.T.O. "Babalon Working," a series of rituals designed to invoke the Thelemic goddess Babalon (the Scarlett Woman, Sacred Whore, and Mother of Abominations). We're not sure what she was supposed to do when she got here, but the whole business certainly made both men infamous in their own right. Still, a woman did appear….

WHAT IS SATANIC SEX MAGIC?

At this point you may ask, just what is Satanic Sex Magic, if not just another occult ritual? The answer is simple. Satanists are not forced to subscribe to any set formula of ritual recitations, elixirs, or what have you to manifest their will. No demons need to be summoned (but that might be fun!), nor circles drawn to "protect" them from the unknown denizens of Hell. Satanic Sex Magic should be used as a potent and pleasurable means to an end – not some intricate, overwrought discipline intended to yield some spooky-ooky "enlightenment." Satanic Sex Magic is about *the* sex. The pure act of having an orgasm (ideally two – one for each partner) releases the energy to change one's mindscape and manifest the "is-to-be."

Of course some Greater ritual magic from *The Satanic Bible* and *Rituals* can indeed be added as a powerful Satanic tool. Warlocks can also add their favorite stimulants to the mix as well as acting out favorite fantasies, perversions, or kinks. Use tried and true aphrodisiacs (see Chapter 6) as enhancements, or concoct your own devil's brew based on the wishes of your partner. We agree with the Marquis de Sade: "Sex is as important as eating or drinking, and we ought to allow the one appetite to be satisfied with as little restraint or false modesty as the other."

Satanic Sex Magic is about getting a result: material gains or the conquest of an exciting new bedmate. If you want to build intensity, hold back your orgasm. Pay attention to your first warning: when the prostatic fluid (pre-cum) starts to leak, slow things down. Think about ugly baseball players or when your next car payment is due. Repeat this cycle as many times as you can. Then, when climax can no longer be postponed, visualize your deepest desires at the moment of orgasm. This is the core of all Sex Magic. Randolph suggested postponing orgasm for six months, but Sex Magic expert Magister David Harris differs: "A healthy abstention is very beneficial, as it allows you to build up a great deal of sexual energy, letting you orgasm more easily. As a general rule, three to five days should be sufficient."

Practicing Randolph's mega-delay theory involves a lot of convoluted nonsense. His books *Eulis! The Story of Love* and *Magic Sexualis: Practices for Magical Power* outlined "steps" for Sex Magic and spells that included *Volancia* (French for "will" or the imaginings of the will), along with *Decretisim* (bending people to your will), *Posism* for receptive positions, and *Tirauclairism*, a form of invocation. So many steps, just to get laid!

And Randolph isn't alone. Just imagine if you had to follow this Lovecraftian magician's long-winded esoteric rigamarole every time you wanted to get some:

> *Even though both the Society of Dark Lily and the Order of Nine Angles differ in their conceptual approach to ritualistic sexual magic, the Order of Nine Angles Rite of Nine Angles provides a prime example of a method of ritualistic Sexual Magic. The sexual nature of the rite may be performed in two ways. Firstly, a Priest and Priestess perform the ritual naked upon an isolated hilltop. The rite itself involves the use of the Sound Magick technique known as vibration, which involves the Priest projecting, in syllables the following words of power: "Nythra Kthunae Atazoth." Thus the syllable "Ny" is sounded for a period of between ten and twenty seconds, then "thra" is sounded for the same period of time, and so on. Such methods of Sound Magick enable the participants to activate hitherto unknown areas of their minds and cause changes in consciousness as though inducing a semi trance-like state. The Priest therefore vibrates these words in the direction of the Priestess who holds a quartz crystal tetrahedron in her palms. After this vibration has been completed, the Priestess lies on the ground, still holding the crystal whilst the Priest performs cunnilingus. When the Priestess is suitably aroused the Priest then begins copulation, during which the Priestess visualizes a gateway situated in the stars above them opening and a black nebulous chaos flowing downwards to the earth.*

> *The second form of the Rite of Nine Angles, known as the Cthonic form, is performed with the addition of a congregation who hold an orgy after the rite, whilst the Priest and Priestess vibrate specific words of power and trained cantors chant a particularly difficult and elaborate Sinister Chant. The energy from the orgy is used to enhance the presencing of the Dark Gods who are then said to manifest. The changes of consciousness that may occur through such a rite can be equated on one level with the creation of the Anti-*

christ, that is, the Satanist who absorbs the power brought forth through the ritual becomes akin to the Antichrist, an individual who embodies the power of the Dark Gods of the Sinister Tradition. Such an individual is considered to be, on a psychic level, a gateway to the abode of the Dark Gods.

Sheesh! Talk about coitus bore-us-to-deathus! As Harris says, Satanic Sex Magic is all about harnessing the power of the orgasm for the purposes of directing that sexual energy out into the universe, towards an intended conquest. Everything else is bullshit.

HOW TO BE AN INCUBUS - RELEASE YOUR BEAST

By the 13th Century, the notion that male Devils (incubi) scoured the night having sex with women in their sleep (especially nuns) was taking hold, to the terror of frightened couples and no doubt the delight of horny women who weren't otherwise gettin' any. By the 17th century, noted demonologist Father Sinistrasi actually described the incubi, calling them Devils who "shape for themselves a body endowed with motion, by means of which body he copulates with the human being."

Unlike the Satanic Witch who exploits her self-conscious modesty (real or imagined) to unleash her lusty Feral Urge, Warlocks are *expected* to be the horny aggressors. To become an incubus, a Warlock need only hone his persona to exhibit his inherent masculinity and project the image that he can deliver what his intended wants (security, excitement, sexual gratification). Warlocks should "shape themselves" into virile beings by projecting their chosen Archetype. Women expect Satanists to be dark and mysterious, so play that card to the hilt. This confidence permeates a woman's subconscious and affects how she thinks of her Warlock by day as well as in her dreams. You have become her incubus!

CASTING YOUR SPELL

When practicing Satanic Sex Magic, the Warlock is no longer a gentleman. Instead, he is the beast Pan, the embodiment of a satyr. A voluptuary, a hedonist, and a libertine. He knows no boundaries; only pure pleasure.

Use the trappings and attire of your chosen Archetype. The gentleman choosing a tuxedo brings sophistication to his lair, setting a suave scenario for his date. The black metal musician tempts his target with his stage-worthy gyrations and the occasional snarl. The intellectual shows off his big brain (or shows her his etchings), making her dizzy and ready to be ravaged.

Use all manner of psychodrama and window dressing, both literal and implied, to create your personal Sex Magic rituals and spells. LaVey provides an excellent "INVOCATION EMPLOYED TOWARDS THE CONJURATION OF LUST" in *The Satanic Bible*, and much more in *The Satanic Rituals*. These are treasure troves of ideas you can customize into Sex Magic scripts to fit your every need. Your mileage may vary, but your satisfaction is limited only by your own diabolical imagination.

No matter your Archetype, be bold with your woman. Take her in your arms and hold her firmly, touching every part of her. Kiss every inch of her skin, put your lips to her ear and whisper blasphemous and obscene ideas. Confess your smoldering lust for her. This is no time for the best friend or the nice guy next door. Unleash your infernal desires. Tell her she is Satan's own and you long to fill her with your demon seed.

Explore her body with your hands, lips, and tongue, probing her with abandon. Revel in the forbidden licks and penetrations. Conjure your filthiest thoughts and desires, and make them real. Your lust will stoke your passion and ignite hers. Tell her what you want to do to her. Compel her to share her deepest desires, then eagerly fulfill them all. The carnal power will reach a fever pitch for both of you.

THE RITUAL CHAMBER

Needless to say, your Ritual Chamber should be outfitted with comfortable bedding or designated areas for sex. But the delightful journey into lust isn't just physical: You must also prep your mind. Let your lustful imaginings run wild. Use filthy language if it helps. Lust is a pillar of the Law of the Forbidden, so using taboos and the perception of evil will charge the atmosphere. Use pornographic images, sex objects and blasphemous toys (crucifix dildos, Jesus butt plugs), BDSM devices and accessories (if so desired), and any sexual imagery that builds the intensity of your experience.

Not long ago, any level of interest in BDSM was considered rare, perverse, shocking, and probably dangerous. Times change and BDSM is so widespread and ho-hum it couldn't shock a third-grader. But whatever you're into, we say embrace that urge! The cathartic use of even the most bizarre fetishes (excluding forced or illegal actions) can easily be defined as Sex Magic in their own right by virtue of the powerful emotions they evoke.

Use as much Satanic imagery as you like including sigils, Baphomets, or pentagrams. Discover which real-world items resonate with your lover and use them. Candles don't need to be black, but they create the best mood lighting, which is key. Also consider using images created by Felicien Rops for example, combining blasphemy with sex. And don't forget the power of music! Classical pieces from Gounod (*Faust*), Wagner (*Ride of the Valkyries, Tannhauser, Tristan and Isolde*), Ravel (*Bolero*), Mussorgsky (*Night On Bald Mountain*), and Berlioz (*Symphonie Fantastique*) are some choice selections with inherently erotic messages to stoke your lustful urges.

Magical locations outside of the usual Ritual Chamber can be particularly powerful conduits for Sex Magic. Heavy flirting and foreplay in public places, followed by a bee-line for the Ritual Chamber can work wonders.

For example, your author participated in an elite and elaborate Church of Satan ritual (replete with naked nun altar) at the infamous Hellfire Caves in West Wycombe, England. Being physically present in an exceptionally magical place sparked an incredible amount of passion among many of the attendees, based on the number of first-hand accounts and obvious real-time responses they shared.

Abandon and lust were palpable at the Caves – no doubt resonating for centuries in that historic den of debauchery. The Caves were a magical laboratory, so to speak, just like the Ritual Chambers that allow magicians to leave the corporeal world and enter a plane of sexual ecstasy.

Harris also points out that despite Hollywood portrayals of "Satanic Ritual Orgies," Warlocks will be most effective in a one-on-one scenario, with a long-time partner. He recommends taking about a year to work out basic sexual operations, freeing your strongest energy for ritualizing. "You should know instinctively where your partner's hot spots are and be able to hit them without losing focus on the point of your specific ritual," he advises.

"Both you and your partner should be very clear on the intention of the ritual before stepping into the ritual chamber, and when the time comes to state your chosen desire, state it passionately and without hesitation or shame. Plant the seed of your intentions firmly into the fertile womb of the universe! This is another reason to practice Sex Magic with someone who knows you intimately: there can be no shame or self-consciousness. The only focus should be on your desire alone."

Harris further instructs that both parties should be fully aroused and ready to commence coitus, instinctively kissing and fondling each other's erogenous zones without losing focus on the rite itself. Harris says: "Two excellent points of focus are your partner's eyes, or if you prefer 'doggy-style,' with both partners facing front, looking at the altar. Maintain contact with the physical sensations of your partner while creating a vision of what you want: a new car, a promotion, a baby, or even to have an unfortunate set of circumstances befall an enemy. This ritual is not about delaying orgasm to increase intensity. When you feel climax approaching, don't hold back. Instead, relax into it and just let it out. Climaxing simultaneously with your partner is ideal but not always possible, so focus instead on both of you releasing a great burst of intense sexual energy into the world. This, combined with the naturally cathartic relief of ritual, should leave both partners pretty exhausted both physically and emotionally. Take a few moments to recover and bask in the afterglow before bringing the ritual to a close and triumphantly shouting, "SO IT IS DONE!"

TAP THE FEMININE URGE

If men are visual, women are certainly verbal. Access her Feral Urge by being a cunning linguist! Chapter 6 showed how words evoke incredible emotions. Here's a particularly graphic bit of porn offered by writer Pagan Slut as an example passage that can be read by the Warlock alone or with his lover to begin the Sex Magic ritual:

> *I told him to lie still while I positioned myself onto his mouth. He knew by my scent it was time to take in my life's essence. Drinking my nectar straight from the cup. Immediately his mouth ravaged my red-soaked pussy. I rose up when I couldn't stand not having him inside me another minute.*

> *His lips smeared with my blood, I kissed him and slowly lowered myself onto him. My fingers in his mouth to taste my mixture of saliva, blood and cum. I adorned my nipples with our paint and threw my head back as I fucked my Satanic beast. Sucking my nipples to near orgasm I begged him to fill me up so we could fully combine. He refused until the time was right.*

> *Moaning deepened, his demon cock stretching me, my pussy forcefully sucking the cum out of him. It was finally time. Exploding inside me he looked into my eyes and made me remember that our intensity had purpose. With a cyclone of liquids brewing inside of me I felt our combined power. I lay down and asked him to feed me our love. As I drank every drop of our cocktail, I felt him slathering me with my blood and licking my stomach. Our magic was just starting.*

Another way to "release the beast" is to blaspheme the Holy Bible. Invoke the historical harlots, the unholy whores: Lilith, Babalon, and Hecate.

Some people who have previously been Christian do find such sorts of blasphemy to be stimulating, and the following passage may even have ushered in their realization that the religion of Jesus was not for them. Those of us who never embraced Christianity tend to find it a bit turgid and confused. But Revelations is used in many horror films as well as a sort of way to validate the "evilness" of what they are portraying, so there may be something to this after all.

WE INVOKE THE UNHOLY WHORES, THE HARLOTS OF HADES AND SURRENDER TO TOTAL LUST. WE MOCK THE BIBLICAL LIES AND PRAISE BABYLON

And there came one of the seven angels which had the seven vials, and talked with me, saying unto me, Come hither; I will shew unto thee the judgment of the great whore that sitteth upon many waters: With whom the kings of the earth have committed fornication, and the inhabitants of the earth have been made drunk with the wine of her fornication. So he carried me away in the spirit into the wilderness: and I saw a woman sit upon a scarlet coloured beast, full of names of blasphemy, having seven heads and ten horns. And the woman was arrayed in purple and scarlet colour, and decked with gold and precious stones and pearls, having a golden cup in her hand full of abominations and filthiness of her fornication: And upon her forehead was a name written, 'Mystery, Babylon the great, the mother of harlots and abominations of the earth.'

Rev 17:1-5

ARTIFICIAL COMPANIONS AND VIRTUAL REALITY – MAGICAL TOOLS FOR THE 21st CENTURY

When Anton LaVey predicted decades ago that artificial companions would become a mainstay of Satanism and the next evolution of man (as well as a huge consumer industry) he no doubt instinctively realized that technology – then in the infancy of creating automaton sex dolls – would allow Satanists to mimic God and create partners for Sex Magic without the baggage and often obnoxious habits of actual humans. And the added benefit would be the ability to produce the most vile, blasphemous, and shocking rituals imaginable without any human concern. "Since almost all creative and/or destructive acts result from the sublimation of sexual drives, the humanoid would preclude sublimation leading to nonsexual but harmful actions," LaVey wrote.

And so it is done! The fembots rise! In 2015, Hollywood gave us an updated blueprint for artificial companions in the sci-fi drama "Ex Machina," featuring more than one very fuckable sex bot. In the last three decades, robot companions have evolved from next-gen blow-up dolls to functional (albeit rudimentary) sex partners, greatly enhancing many Sex Magic rituals.

Forbes recently reported that Virtual Reality (VR) and sex robots are going to merge. Granted, this form of masturbatory magic isn't nearly as much fun as *bumping pee pees*, but it's still a viable means to the orgasmic end.

More of LaVey's predictions are being confirmed every day. By 2050, love with robots will be as common as human love, according to predictions by A.I. expert David Levy in his book *Love and Sex With Robots*. He even believes people will be able to marry their fembots by the year 2050! Hail Anton LaVey!

The RealDoll company (appropriately named Abyss Creations) has been making life-like sex dolls since 1996. "They are currently developing an A.I. head that can be switched out with the static heads of their current dolls. As delightfully morbid as that sounds, the A.I. head's purpose is, according to RealDoll's founder and CEO Matt McMullen, to 'arouse someone on an emotional and intellectual level, beyond the physical,'" Forbes reported.

Called "Realbotix," RealDoll's new head technology will have realistic eye contact, blinking, smiling, and allow manipulation of the mouth. The head is due in 2017 and can be placed on existing RealDoll bodies for a cost of about $10,000. The company's latest creation (Taffy) "RealDoll2, Body A" has silicone skin (as LaVey predicted decades ago) and steel joints, and costs about $7,000. Options include different faces, hairstyles and 11 different styles of labia for those who want variety in their vaginas.

True Companion, another humanoid sex robot manufacturer offers up RoxxxyGold 16 for $7,000, with a heartbeat and built-in orgasms. Perfect for last minute rituals! The creators of these dolls believe that within a few years the sex bots will be capable of "expressing the illusion of emotions," according to a 2016 article in *Men's Health* magazine.

What's more, Stanford University scientists used a robot from Aldebaran Robotics to perform a study in which the participants fondled the humanoid's private parts. When they did, the arousal section of the volunteers' brains lit up, indicating that the humans got turned on by the robot. The human response to a non-human partner suggests that incorporating a fembot into Sex Magic may be all the Warlock needs to create powerful rituals and spells!

VIRTUAL SEX MAGIC

For Warlocks whose budgets won't allow for a humanoid (although prices are expected to drop considerably with time), another Sex Magic alternative is virtual reality (VR). Albeit not as tactile, VR nevertheless is a version of remote sex and can be convenient for spur of the moment workings. In 2016, users wear a headset (Google Cardboard or Oculus Rift), large goggles uploaded with specially designed digital programming like VirtuaDolls and VR Bangers (as in every new technology, porn leads the way) that allows the user to "virtually" experience sex.

The technology is quickly advancing. VR is also being linked with fembots and other devices that can be attached to the penis for a total experience. In fact, RealDoll is working on a Realbotix Siri-like app that will allow users to design their own personal sex avatars to appear on a computer screen, tablet, or phone, to fulfill any desire they dictate.

Playboy recently featured inventor and futurist Raymond Kurzweil, Google's director of engineering. Kurzweil created the first OCR (optical character recognition) system and electronic music keyboard synthesizer. Now he's shifted his vision to remote sex. The guru, who also founded Singularity University research institute, predicts that people will not only be able to have sex "together" from different locations, but will have the ability to digitally manipulate their and their partners' identities. If that's not god-like and Satanic what is?

Of course Warlocks still need to heed the fundamentals of Satanic ritual, even when using new technology. Whether seeking a material gains or summoning a real-life sex partner, the Warlock must have a strong emotional tie to his fembot or virtual partner in order to create an orgasm powerful enough for his magic to work.

PATIENCE

Results from Sex Magic can manifest immediately or not be evident for days or even months. Much depends on the intensity of the energy produced and the will of the participants. So be patient. The upside is if you don't see immediate results, it's always pleasurable to try, try again! If nothing else, partners will celebrate carnal pleasures and a cathartic release of anxiety – which truly is magic of the highest order!

Not buying it?

During one particularly intense lovemaking session (including many blasphemous outbursts and invocations to his Infernal Majesty), I defined my intention to have my dark-haired partner as a major part of my life. At the moment of ecstasy, I held this image clearly in my mind, as *le petit mort* enveloped us. To my surprise, instead of the usual *apres* cuddle or cigarette, the lady promptly turned her back to me and moved to the other side of the bed. Whatever she meant, I could only interpret it as "Ok, I'm done. Let yourself out."

Needless to say, this put a damper on the session and a dent in my ego. Although everything afterward was quite pleasant, I still couldn't understand the hasty uncoupling. Usually the man wants to take a nap, smoke, or get back to his to-do list. I chalked it up to "just her way," and wondered if perhaps I was being used as a plaything (still not a bad way to spend an evening!).

So what does that have to do with Sex Magic, you ask? Well, when we parted, I expected a "see ya" and to never cross paths again. We corresponded… for a while, cordial and somewhat romantic, but distant at best. But what do you know? About a year later the girl reached out and the whole thing reignited – hotter and heavier than ever. So my point is… sometimes your best magic just takes time.

warlock wisdom

- The goal of Satanic Sex Magic is to visualize what you desire at the moment of orgasm – everything else is window dressing.

- Occultnik Sex Magic may be spooky and amusing, but it's basically bullshit.

- Unleash your Beast – bolster your Archetype – be her incubus.

- Release her Feral Urge and inner slut with your passionate words.

- Adorn your Ritual Chamber with shocking or blasphemous items to induce dark desires.

- Engage your mind with your most erotic fantasies and fulfill them when possible.

- Focus your thoughts on your desired goals at the moment of ejaculation.

- Use humanoids or fembots to replace humans if you desire.

THE GAY SATANIC WARLOCK

It should come as no surprise that a significant number of Satanists are gay men. Occult lore is filled with same-sex loving magicians from Crowley's "sex magick" affair with Victor Neuberg in his "Paris Working," to cross dresser Simon Ganneau, mentor of Eliphas Levi, who believed in the unity of the sexes, to even Ol' Scratch himself, who's no stranger to every sort of dalliance in his eternal pursuit of sinful souls. The belief in magic, especially the demonic, calls to those commonly disenfranchised, different, bullied, bashed, or battered, enticing them with the promise of a unique power to wield against their foes.

But what may not be so readily understood is that under the skin, a man is a man and a Warlock is a Warlock. Regardless of sexual proclivity or gender identity, the driving forces of the male animal (XY chromosome, DNA markers, and brain structure) determine how men act. We are ALL basically hunters in search of sexual variety, and to call many of us promiscuous is a gross understatement.

After countless interviews and discussions with Warlocks, both gay and straight, as well as with men aligned with the tenets of Satanism, this notion is even more pronounced and only reinforces the undeniable conclusion that *pleasure* is the ultimate goal for all men. Satanists see no distinct differences (or biases) in how the flesh is appeased, as long as satisfaction is achieved.

Satanism appeals to many non-straight men because of its acceptance of all sexual preferences and celebration of their diversity as even more proof of man's true carnality. We are all living proof that the male beast simply cannot be pigeonholed into one "right" sexual appetite. Men crave variety in their sex lives and Satanism affords them the opportunity to indulge their fantasies to the fullest, relieving them of the restrictions that otherwise constrain the herd, always managing to separate them from whatever turns them on. Satanism means freedom!

The best-known research into the wide spectrum of sexual preferences comes from pioneering sex researcher Dr. Alfred Kinsey, going back as far as 1948. Certainly a de facto Satanist, Kinsey's groundbreaking work gave the world the famous "Kinsey Scale" published in *Sexual Behavior in the Human Male*. The scale rates a person's sexual proclivity from 0 to 6 (0 being exclusively heterosexual and 6 being exclusively gay), with an additional category of X (no socio-sexual contacts or relations).

The Scale clearly showed that most men have a wide range of sexual appetites—some very heterosexual, some very homosexual, and quite a few somewhere in between (the ancient Romans illustrated this point quite nicely... and had a helluva a good time doing it!).

Kinsey's research shook the very foundation of common culture at the time when he also revealed that one in three people has had at least an incidental gay sexual experience, recognizing that man's carnal appetites run much deeper than the accepted and restrictive societal and religious commandments. About 30% of men aged 16-55 reported having a gay experience at some point, according to Kinsey. And although we now know his subjects may not have been clear indicators of the "average" population (back then the only people who would consent to be interviewed were the sexually adventurous, met by Kinsey in bars, many of them gay bars at that), the Kinsey Reports are still studied and respected.

I find it personally gratifying (and so Satanic!) that gay men played a key role in this groundbreaking research. Every time a homophobe cringes to hear that gays are a significant percentage of the population, thank a pioneering Sodomite!

Fast forward to 2016, where in her Philly.com article, Brooke Wells, a social psychologist at Widener University's Center for Human Sexuality Studies said, "People over time are reporting more same-sex sexual experiences than ever before."

And a survey of nearly 34,000 people (between 1973 and 2014) conducted by faculty from Widener, Florida Atlantic and San Diego State Universities found that the number of U.S. adults who said they had at least one same-sex sexual partner doubled between the early 1990s and the early 2010s, from 3.6 to 8.7 percent for women and from 4.5 to 8.2 percent for men. Bisexual behavior rose from 3.1 to 7.7 percent, accounting for most of the change.

What's more, the percentage of respondents who said they believed same-sex behavior was "not wrong at all" rose dramatically, from 11 percent in 1973 and 13 percent in 1990 to 49 percent in 2014. An impressive amount of progress in a mere 41 years!

In fact, gay men have more sex than just about anyone, simply because men have far fewer prerequisites than women when it comes to choosing a partner. Researchers John and Julia Schwartz Gottman point out in their book *The Man's Guide to Women* that women are predominantly concerned with emotional closeness before they'll permit any carnal coupling. Men in general will stick their dicks into anything young and hot. Gay men, minus that resistance from a female partner, will have sex in the shower at the gym if someone else is present and cooperative. Conversely, lesbian couples have *less* sex on average, due to those same female requirements.

This growing social and moral acceptance of gay sex doesn't surprise Satanists. Why deny such a prominent component of the human psyche? We are happy to see more people finally unafraid to explore their forbidden sexuality, something we've lustily been doing for more than 50 years. Meanwhile, researchers are uncovering so much data that many sexologists believe the Kinsey Scale is not comprehensive enough to cover all known sexual identity issues. They suggest that sexual identity involves at least three different spectra, sexual orientation being only one of them (two others being biological sex and gender identity).

Want an example? I interviewed two prominent Warlocks for this book, both of whom always struck me as straight as could be. Neither showed any signs of homosexual leanings. We'd cursed, hoisted drinks, and commented on this broad's boobs or that babe's butt. I have pretty good "gaydar" for a straight man, and nothing moved the meter. But after reading their questionnaires, I discovered that one of the fellows – a female-loving stud by all appearances and actions – had unapologetically dabbled in same-sex trysts as a young man. The other prefers cross-dressing, and although he enjoys women more, is not opposed to transgender sexual relationships.

I wasn't at all shocked; more like pleasantly surprised to see Satanism create confidence and comfort with their true carnal selves.

Once again, Anton LaVey was far ahead of the pack in understanding what really makes people tick, as evident in the growing number of LGBTQ people embracing Satanism in all its rational beauty.

This book is for and about men. In the planning stage, I naturally intended to dedicate a chapter to the Gay Warlock. I reasoned that maleness is universal, so advice and information could easily translate to any man, making it unnecessary to segregate the Gay Satanic Warlock from his straight brothers. But in numerous discussions with accomplished Gay Warlocks both inside and outside of the Church, it became clear that some sexual identities were omitted (bisexual, transgender, queer), and that a discussion of the Gay Warlock needed to include numerous subtleties, sub-categories, fetishes, and sexual tastes that only a Gay Warlock himself could properly address. Niche interests and fetishes continue to expand and evolve. More importantly, Gay men take their sexual delights very seriously and are some of the most epicurean when it comes to selecting partners (and porn!).

We quickly realized that the nuances of non-straight life would require more than just one chapter.

As prominent Gay Warlock Magister Joe Netherworld noted earlier, today's Gay Warlock creates his own reality, accepting the villain as role model. He offers the wisdom only a Gay Warlock can. "Learn some lost and taboo history; apply some arcane and occult philosophy to your daily life," in order to gain an advantage in the mundane world.

And although much of this book will be useful to Gay Warlocks in their quest for identity and learning a few male "tricks of the trade,"

I've decided *The Gay Satanic Warlock* must be its own book – as Netherworld described it, a "Book of Homosexual Shadows." Research is now underway and the book will be written by a Gay Warlock, with yours truly as a co-author and consultant.

Other-gender Warlocks (any who identify with the LGBTQ or "other than straight" communities) will also benefit from a book dedicated to their smaller but ever growing and accepted sexual lifestyle. And certainly the many Warlocks who call themselves "pansexual" (choosing to enjoy the fruits of all people) will also be represented.

In the interim, and in keeping with true Satanic acceptance of all things carnal, it is only right to share the wisdom of a select few exemplary Gay Warlocks. Following is first-hand insight into what attracts the Gay man to Satanism, opinions on the major differences/similarities to Straight Warlocks, and what some Gay Warlocks see on the horizon.

GAY WARLOCKS SPEAK OUT

Reverend Lee M. Crowell, a prominent and successful attorney from the D.C. area, says he discovered *The Satanic Bible* in his mother's closet as a teenager and has never looked back. His attraction to Satanism resulted from a feeling of "not fitting in" with any particular group. The injustices of being "different," Crowell says, sparked his interest in Satanism, particularly because of the Church's acceptance of those who are alienated elsewhere.

"My understanding of the human animal and acknowledgement of the need to fight resonated with me. The tenets of Satanism pierced my mind and ignited that black flame in my heart. Someone saw the world the way I did! I found comfort in knowing I was not alone. Isolated not only in my view of the world and the injustices I saw plaguing everyday life with no ramifications, I believed I had finally discovered the framework to forge a path to greatness. Satanism showed me that if it were not my sexual identity, society would find another way to try to marginalize me, subjugate me, and otherwise ensure I 'knew my place,'" he says.

Crowell adds that the similarities between the Gay and Straight Warlock can be identified in the anti-establishment and counterculture personality that flows through them. Though sexual preference may differ, general disdain for society as a whole appears to be a constant. He believes each Warlock seeks out that subculture where he can bond and fulfill whatever social need arises, whether it be music, art, sexual eccentricity, or pontificating about a shared religious philosophy. In his case it was Satanism.

Warlock Aden Ardennes, author of *Militant Eroticism* and publisher of *HORNS*, a Satanic gay adult magazine, says he's "as masculine as The Riddler," employing Lesser Magic as the "bow and arrow" on his hunt to fulfill his desires, both professional and sexual. He says he's found true acceptance in "the Devil's Church," never just tolerance, but that the organization also demands productivity. "The attitude [of the Church] was always 'Wonderful, you can put penises in your backdoor; can you do anything else?'"

He sees no need for a rainbow Baphomet flag, because homosexuals have always been bound for Hell with the rest of the Sodomites. "I've simply come home. Anton LaVey made it clear that my bedroom doings are absolutely irrelevant. I think that is part of my love for Satanism, the Dark Lord requires nothing from me but that which I seek, fulfilled. Satan requires one to be himself, without compromise."

A veteran Satanic confidant who greatly contributed to the "aha" moment that Warlocks are men first and their sexual preferences second, Magister Neil Smith noted that when comparing and contrasting the behaviors of heterosexual and homosexual males, we find more to unite us than divide us. He says all men share common ground in terms of how the male mind works – the sensory mechanisms of stimulation, the factors that engage their interests and motivate them to pursue the object of their desire, regardless of which body parts are getting the action.

Smith says a Gay Warlock might also be attracted to Satanism if he identifies with the atheistic philosophy most Satanists embrace. He may share the epicurean approach to living life, or the understanding that society is stratified, not egalitarian. In short, Gay Warlocks are often attracted to Satanism the same way anyone else is.

"What differentiates a Gay Warlock from a Straight Warlock is the people who interest him and stimulate him sexually," Smith explains. "The fact that Satanism is absolutely open to any form of sexual expression (as long as it excludes minors and non-consenting partners) is probably more attractive to gay men (and women) than to straight folks, because heterosexuals don't have to deal with biases, bigotry, and intolerance.'"

Another illuminating fact Smith points out is the contrast between straight males and gay males in most societies when it comes to the restraints on sexual behavior. He believes that despite the increased interest in "open marriages" and polyamory, the majority of straight men are expected to fit into restrictive paradigms like faithful husband, good provider, and responsible parent. As much as it may cause conflict with his sexual nature, the straight male is also expected to be sexually active ("faithful") only with his wife. If he strays and gets caught, he is branded a philanderer (although he may get a few winks of approval when out with the boys). If he keeps his dalliances discreet, as has been the case for centuries, no one is officially the wiser, and the standing and reputation of the family and spouse remain untarnished.

"Homosexual men, who've always been on the fringes of mainstream society, don't have such behavioral expectations. There are no societal norms because we are not included in the life scripts of mainstream society. We have no external expectations of fidelity, because there's no bloodline to protect. Because gay men are less restricted by such codes, we can be more sexually active without having to be discreet," Smith says.

Aside from sexual preference, what Gay Warlocks perceive as the distinct differences from their straight brothers may not be revealing, but they nonetheless offer insight as to how Satanism transcends gender boundaries and strengthens the bond among all Warlocks.

Crowell believes Satanism connects the young gay male to his power through the use of Greater Magic. The power of ritual fills a void created by discrimination that often severely limits teen love experiences (and the emotional roller coaster rides they provide). Sexuality notwithstanding, this is a feeling all Warlocks who identify as *different* can certainly appreciate.

Ardennes agrees that the most significant difference is obviously in "the change of quarry," but points out that if the strategy is to charm one's prey and manipulate them towards a desired end, there is no real difference between homosexual and heterosexual Warlocks.

Concerning the use of Lesser Magic, Ardennes said the differences lie with the genders being exploited, utilizing social stereotypes, and type-casting oneself based on how others typically perceive a gay Warlock. "There is no gender difference to exploit, we [Gay Warlocks] are stereotyped by the heterosexual culture, and how we perceive men through that 'rainbow tint' is very different. Everyone at the table is playing poker, except some of us happen to be from Mars."

He also points out that gay subcultures mostly revolve around sexual interests and aesthetics, so if a Warlock sees himself as a LaVey 3 o'clock, with an interest in being a Sir/Dom in the hyper masculine BDSM world, although he has his work cut out for him, it's not an impossible goal because the target is still another man. In contrast, the heterosexual Warlock is seducing a woman, intrinsically different from himself, meaning he must use a different kind of magic to appeal to her needs. Ardennes likens it to hunting big cats in the mountains versus on a savannah.

"We both have our aims and choose the best path to their achievement, by almost any means required. We both seek pleasure and satisfaction in all areas of our lives and we've both sworn our loyalty to Satan, our names right there on the dotted line in our Luciferian pact. Our games and the specifics of our magic may differ, but at the end of the day we're both trying to score some ass," Ardennes says.

Crowell believes that man can choose to answer the carnal call with constructive or destructive behaviors. He says as a Gay Warlock, the choice is always toward refinement and betterment of oneself, through Satanism or some professional endeavor.

"The White Anglo Saxon Protestant (WASP) of the 1950s was once the dominant force in our society. It was not only expected that a WASP would get every promotion, but that a happy home life with a wife and children went along with that package – no white picket fence, no keys to the executive washroom. As the rapid change in cultural and social dynamics seems to indicate, the details of one's personal life are becoming less and less important. The future of the Gay Warlock is bright because now professional life and private life remain separate. You can work with someone for 10 years and not know if they are married or have children. This shift in society's expectation that they have *the right to know* has taken the heat off every non-conformist, not just homosexuals. Finally having privacy has created an environment where an openly Gay Satanist is able to work in an executive branch of government without risking his job security," Crowell says.

This new paradigm has fostered opportunity for advancement based on achievement with little concern for personal ethics/morality. Crowell cautions, however, that the gay community must continue to stick together, particularly Satanists and Warlocks, who will continue to manifest the kind of changes others can barely dream of.

Warlock Lucien Stanton DeVille on the differences between Gay Warlocks and Straight Warlocks:

"Well, outside of the obvious fact of our chosen partners, I found myself asking… *Hmmmm. What is a 'Gay Warlock?' And what is a 'Straight Warlock?'* I never once linked sexual identities to any title in any way, with the exception of how Satanism pertained to me specifically in my own life. Which led me to the ultimate question, *What is a Satanist?'* Honestly, I couldn't think of a thing that (at least in my own experience, which is all that matters to me) would delineate Gay from Straight Warlocks.

The crux of LaVey's philosophies is to live as an individualist, being the best that you can be in this life that you know as YOURS. To not flow with the 'Herd Mentality,' taking everything without question and gaining acceptance through conformity.

From this I took what I needed and left the rest, forming what was to become my version apropos to my life. If we all followed Anton LaVey's practices to the letter, would we not be just another Herd?

I'm sure this is something he would not have wanted nor condoned. This again proved to me that 'Satanists are born, not cultivated' and 'Great minds think alike', but even more importantly, Satanists think differently. I even disagree with a number of the good Doktor's takes on things, for which I believe he would be proud of me."

So... What are the differences between Gay Warlocks and Straight Warlocks?

The answer is NOTHING and EVERYTHING, because we are all Satanists, each in our own individual way, again, making us a group of individualists. We are indeed the very antithesis of a herd, as we share no ONE mentality.

CHAPTER NINE

THE HIGH PRIESTESS SPEAKS!

**"The truly 'liberated' female is the compleat witch,
who knows both how to use and enjoy men."
Anton LaVey. *The Satanic Witch***

Many outstanding Witches contributed to the writing of this book, and I am truly grateful to every one of them. One voice shines above all others, though, warranting a chapter all her own. Of course I am referring to the alluring and always outspoken High Priestess of The Church of Satan herself, Magistra Peggy Nadramia.

Our High Priestess has been front and center for Satanism for decades, flicking away the slings and arrows of her detractors like so many sand fleas. She and High Priest Peter H. Gilmore have piloted the Church into the 21st century, stronger and more vibrant than ever, driven by their deeply burning Hellfire.

A confidant to many a Satanic Witch, HP Nadramia has also counseled many a needy and bewildered Warlock, setting them straight on how to live as true beasts of the field... in other words, "using their heads for more than a hat rack."

So many Warlocks owe their key victories or accolades to Nadramia's rapier wit, razor-sharp intellect, and on-point advice. Her affection for Warlocks is evident here, expressed as always in her frank, enlightening, and entertaining style.

If you take nothing else from this book, heed the High Priestess's words. They are the straight Satanic dope, direct from the Witch with all the secrets. She holds the keys to the gates of Hell and can school any man in the dark and decadent arts!

Magister Robert Johnson: How do you define the 21st Century Satanic Warlock?

High Priestess Peggy Nadramia: The 21st Century Satanic Warlock is the culmination of decades of Satanic principles and ideas, resulting in the epitome of male attraction, effectiveness, and power. He is completely comfortable in his flesh, no matter what its age or shape, because he knows what he has to offer. He literally "has it going on," in his career, his financial situation, his social life, his interests, and recreation. Women are naturally attracted to him like moths to a flame, and not necessarily for sex: he's fun to be around, he knows how to get things done and his reflected light shines brightly on anyone who is lucky enough to be in his circle. When he sees a woman he wants for bedtime fun, friendship, career advantages, or all three, he pursues her and wins her, or brushes off defeat with a jaunty wave, because he's confident another woman will be along shortly. His smile is warm, but his self-confidence is titanium steel.

MRJ: What makes him unique as compared to non-Satanists?

HPPN: A Satanic Warlock, as opposed to any other successful sexy man, lives by Satanic principles. He hunts his quarry, completely conscious that he's using his wits and wiles, feeling not a shred of "guilt" when a woman succumbs to his charms – because he knows he's just provided the means by which she's "allowed" herself to join in the fun. Responsibility to the responsible means the Satanic Warlock knows exactly what he's getting into when he seduces a woman. His guiding dictum is *lead her into temptation*, never forcing her into something she genuinely doesn't want – no fun in that for a true Warlock.

MRJ: How would Anton LaVey feel about today's Warlock?

HPPN: Dr. LaVey would have a lot of sympathy for today's Warlock, I believe. Being a rapscallion in the 21st century is an uphill climb; a real tough row to hoe. Men in general are constantly being pushed around and defanged, and the slightest whiff of male aggression gets the evildoer pilloried in the court of social media. Nevertheless, women are still interested in clever villains, muscled heroes, Romeos, and Don Juans, and Dr. LaVey would be watching to see how his Warlocks execute these roles while staying one step ahead of the PC police. On the other hand, he might ENJOY seeing them give the one-finger salute and tick a few people off. At the end of the day, Dr. LaVey always respected success over failure, no matter what the endeavor.

MRJ: What is the single most important personality trait a Warlock must possess?

HPPN: It is absolutely essential for the Satanic Warlock to display confidence in himself, in his own value, ability, and attractiveness. This is not to say that he should be boastful or make himself the focus of every conversation; this actually conveys the opposite. My admittedly lowbrow vision of what the Satanic Warlock should project is the character of Mike Damone in "Fast Times at Ridgemont High." A Satanic Warlock must convey "The Attitude," which is that wherever you are, *that's* the place to be. With his presence alone, the Satanic Warlock has made things great. And if a young lady fails to smell his qualifications, he is completely untroubled. He has *The Attitude*. Satanic Warlocks must cultivate The Attitude.

MRJ: What makes a Warlock appealing to women?

HPPN: Remember all those old cartoons and illustrations where a devil appears on someone's shoulder, encouraging that person to "be naughty?" Most of the time, the devil wants you to do the exact thing you're already considering. The Satanic Warlock must represent and embody that devil. He has to make a woman see that he has a big bag of fun, naughty tricks they can play together, and that he's materialized solely to deliver that adventure. She can abstain, but he will take a dim view of that. The Satanic Warlock dangles a unique and enticing experience, maybe even laced with a bit of danger, and if she wants his approval, she will take the bait.

MRJ: What is the Warlock's most important overall attribute?

HPPN: A Satanic Warlock has to be happy with himself. He has to be satisfied with the person he is and the place he occupies in the world. This is different from self-confidence (see above), although it is certainly what inspires it. Ambition, goals, striving for perfection, these can all co-exist alongside self-satisfaction. No woman is attracted to that hangdog guy who whines about his car, his apartment, the sparseness of his beard or his upset stomach. Even a man living in one room (with wonderful accessories) and driving an old (but well-maintained) car can have a plan to do better, moving ever forward with contentment for his current situation and never complaining.

MRJ: What do you feel many Warlocks lack (if anything)?

HPPN: If a man has successfully employed Satanic principles of attraction to the extent that I'd acknowledge him as a true Satanic Warlock, he shouldn't lack for much. But a general observation I might make is that Satanic Warlocks could be doing a bit more self-scrutiny in the hope of ramping up their game. Some Warlocks also lack initiative; they seem to have missed the point about the procurement of a proper mate being a PURSUIT. Women aren't going to come to you unless you put yourself in the right place at the right time.

MRJ: How can today's Warlock improve himself?

HPPN: From my observations, a Warlock who desires to engage in the chase can do better in several areas. He has to assess his strengths and weaknesses mercilessly, and he has to make improvements accordingly. He has to clear his vision of many pre-determined standards of beauty and sexual attraction and decide what kind of woman really interests him. He has to understand that while sexual conquests and a varied and robust career between the sheets may be his main focus, he may also want to pursue women as friends, business partners, and clients. He should know his talents can be employed there as well. And a true Satanic Warlock must remember that he doesn't work in a vacuum: his success can sometimes be contingent on his relationships with other men (Satanic or otherwise), so he must be careful and considerate when working his magic around them.

MRJ: What must a Warlock do to succeed?
HPPN: A Warlock's success is directly related to what he has to offer and his realistic perception of what that actually is. In the animal kingdom, males attract their desired females by displaying strength or beautiful plumage, or by digging the safest, warmest dens, or by providing the best food, or by decorating their nests with the shiniest objects. A Warlock has to take a look at where he excels, where he needs improvement, and act on that. Be realistic. Make changes. Get out there and find your Satanic female counterpart. This is no time for boyhood fantasies or the "spiritual pipe dreams" of sexual youth! This is vital existence in the Here and Now.

MRJ: How do you define the Gay Warlock and what makes him unique/different from straight Warlocks (if at all)?
HPPN: Not being a man, or subject to the attentions of gay men, my answer should be taken with an overstuffed purse full of salt, and probably says more about me than it does about gay Warlocks. But since you asked, a Gay Warlock is a man who enjoys having sex with men, and employs Satanic principles in both his sexual and non-sexual pursuits. Gay culture, the traditional "types," roles and icons, can be pretty different from those in the heterosexual world, but I think the need to project confidence, to be realistic about who really attracts you and what you have to offer, all still apply to both Gay Warlocks and Lesbian Witches. A Gay Warlock may need to be even more conscious about the real effect his behavior and appearance are having on those around him when he's out on the prowl, as crossed signals can not only waste his efforts, but prove dangerous in the wrong circles.

AFTERWORD

And so it is done!

An actual book! A manual for today's Satanic Warlock, a companion to Anton LaVey's *Satanic Witch*, for sorcerers extraordinaire – the culmination of years of Satanic research, put to paper in an age when the joy of reading is unfortunately waning. But therein lies the magic of Satanic principle, as many Warlocks still cherish the written word, relishing the paper, binding and even the smell of rare old books. Warlocks clamored for a book like this – a real book – to carry with them and display in their bookcases with the rest of their Satanic canon.

What I have shared is by no means everything the Warlock needs to know. It's not a textbook, but it is a *grimoire;* a launching-off point designed to show the 21st century Warlock who he is and what he can accomplish. Anything left unsaid was intended to motivate the reader to do what every Warlock *should* be doing – get off his ass and find the answers for himself! The secret to living life as a truly realized Satanist is *doing*. Doing is the mechanism of magic. It opens doors and makes connections. Doing is Lesser Magic. Creating is Lesser Magic. Producing is Lesser Magic. Giving birth to something is truly Satanic because it changes the environment that birthed it. Adding something to the *zeitgeist* makes the Warlock immortal and elevates him above the "lives of quiet desperation."

Fifty years into the society founded by Anton LaVey, Warlocks must embrace what defines us as the Alien Elite. We must demonstrate in word and deed what it is to be a Warlock. We must strengthen our allegiance to the Church of Satan and quash its detractors. Speak out against the poseurs and those jealous of the pedigree and accomplishments of the Church citizenry. Nurture and love your beautiful Witches.

I leave you with the "9 Ways of the Warlock" – succinct statements that codify the new band of Hellfire born. Hail to all you rogues, libertines, villains, hedonists, rascals, scoundrels, tricksters, and dashing devils. You are the new Black Guard of Warlocks guarding the Gates of Hell for the next generations of Satanism. You are the keepers of the carnal and the celebrants of the flesh!

Finally, I ask you to continue to visit TheSatanicWarlock.com. The new, dynamic website will provide more in-depth information on life, health, seduction, and the challenge of being a man among men. Along with some pleasing pulchritude of course!

And as I always like to say, "…Ahhhh, it's good to be bad!"

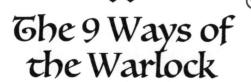

The 9 Ways of the Warlock

Warlocks walk on two legs, but live as though they have four.

Warlocks live fiercely and love lustfully.

Warlocks use confidence as their calling card.

Warlocks are gentlemen first, but behave as beasts to their enemies.

Warlocks produce rather than pontificate. Create rather than crow.

Warlocks live by magic, not simply *practice* magic.

Warlocks would rather be desired than liked.

Warlocks use seduction as a weapon on the battlefield of the mind.

Warlocks seek power because power buys freedom.

SELECT BIBLIOGRAPHY

Anand, Margo, *The Art of Sexual Ecstasy.* Los Angeles: Jeremy P. Tarcher, Inc., 1989

Arthur, Gavin, *The Circle Of Sex.* New York: University Books Inc., 1966

Ashe, Geoffrey, *The Hell-Fire Clubs.* England: Sutton Publishing, 2005

Atkinson, William Walker, *Mind-Power. The Secret Of Mental Magic,* Illinois: Yogi Publication Society, 1940

Barton, Blanche, *The Secret Life Of A Satanist.* Washington: Feral House, 1990, 1992

Black, Jason S., Hyatt, Christopher S., *Pacts With The Devil.* Arizona: New Falcon Publications, 1993

Bridges, John, *How To Be A Gentleman.* Tennessee: Rutledge Hill Press, 1998

Bryan, James, *The Fine Art Of Seduction.* Vermont: Gallant publishing, 1986

Cavendish, Richard, *The Black Arts.* New York: Perigee Books, 1967

Chartham, Robert, *What Turns Women On.* New York: Ballantine Books, 1974

Crowley, Aleister, *Magick In Theory and Practice.* New Jersey: Castle Books, 1991

Ellis, Havelock, *Psychology Of Sex.* New York: Mentor Books, 1933, 1938

Fast, Julius & Bernstein, Meredith, *Sexual Chemistry.* New York: M. Evans & Co., Inc., 1983

Finlay, Anthony, *Demons! The Devil, Possession & Exorcism.* England: Blandford Cassell, 1999

Flynn, Errol, *My Wicked, Wicked Ways.* New York: Berkley Publishing, 1959

Gilmore, Peter H., *The Satanic Scriptures.* Maryland: Scapegoat Publishing, 2007

Gottman, John & Gottman, Julia Schwartz, *The Man's Guide to Women.* New York: Rodale, 2016

Gray, John, *Men Are From Mars, Women Are From Venus*. New York: Quill, Harper Collins, 2004

Greene, Robert, *The 48 Laws Of Power*. New York: Penguin Group, 1998

Greene, Robert, *The Art Of Seduction*. New York: Penguin Group, 2001

Greene, Robert & Cent, 50, *The 50th Law*. New York: Harper Collins, 2009

Hamill, Pete, *Why Sinatra Matters*. Boston: Back Bay Books, 1998

Hefner, Hugh M., *Hef's Little Black Book*. New York: Harper Entertainment, 2004

Kinsey, Alfred, *Sexual Behavior In The Human Male*. Indiana: D.B. Saunders Company, 1948

Kinsey, Alfred, Pomeroy Wardell B., et al, *Sexual Behavior In The Human Female*. Indiana: D.B. Saunders Company, 1953

Lang, Doe, *The Charisma Book*. New York: Wyden Books, 1980

Laurent, Emile & Nagour, Paul, *Magica Sexualis*. The Netherlands: Fredonia Books, 2003

LaVey, Anton, *Satan Speaks*, California: Feral House, 1998

LaVey, Anton, *The Compleat Witch*, New York; Dodd, Mead & Company, 1970

LaVey, Anton, *The Devil's Notebook*, California: Feral House, 1992

LaVey, Anton, *The Satanic Bible*. New York: Avon Books, 1969

LaVey, Anton, *The Satanic Rituals*, New York: Avon Books, 1972

LaVey, Anton, *The Satanic Witch*. California: Feral House, 1989

Leary, Mark, *Understanding the Mysteries of Human Behavior – Course Guidebook*, Virginia: The Great Courses, 2012

Leigh, Wendy, *What Makes A Man G.I.B.*, New York: Signet Book, 1979

"M", *The Way To Become The Sensuous Man*, New York: Dell Publishing, 1971

Machiavelli, Niccolo, *The Prince and The Discourses*, New York: Random House, 1940

Medway, Gareth J., *Lure Of The Sinister, The Unnatural History of Satanism*, New York: New York University Press, 2001

Morganstern, Michael, *How To Make Love To A Woman*, New York:

Clarkson N. Potter Inc., 1982

Morganstern, Michael, *A Return To Romance*, New York: Harper & Roe Publishers, 1984

Mortensen, William & Dunham, George, *The Command To Look*, California: Feral House, 2014

Moylan, Brian, *Dad Bod is a Sexist Atrocity*, Time.com/3846828/dad-bod-is-a-sexist-atrocity/, May 5, 2015

Newell, Walter R., *What is A Man*, New York: Regan Books, 2000

Pearson, Mackenzie, *Why Girls Love The Dad Bod*, TheOdysseyOnline.com/dad-bod, March 30, 2015

Shorter, Edward, *Written In The Flesh, History Of Desire*, Canada: University of Toronto Press, 2005

Stanford, Peter, *The Devil, A Biography*, New York: Henry Holt & Co. Inc., 1996

Steele, Don R., *Body Language Secrets*, California: Steel Balls Press, 1999

Steele, Don R., *Date Young Women For Men Over 35*, California: Steel Balls Press, 1999 Strauss, Neil, *The Game*, New York: Regan Books, 2005

Sutin, Lawrence, *Do What Thou Wilt, A Life Of Aleister Crowley*, New York: St. Martin's Press, 2000

Romassi, Rollo, *The Rational Male*, Nevada: Counterflow Media LLC, 2013

Tracy, Brian & Arden, Ron, *The Power Of Charm*, New York: American Management Association, 2006

Weber, Eric, *How To Pick Up Girls*, New Jersey: Symphony Press, 1970

Zeehme, Bill, *The Way You Wear Your Hat, Frank Sinatra and The Lost Art Of Livin'*, New York: Harper Collins, 1997

People are *still* talking...

The long-awaited authorized male companion to The Satanic Witch is finally here. And what an amazingly insightful and useful book this is! Gain direct insights into the worldview of the true Satanic Warlock. Discover the practical tricks and tools used by Satanic Warlocks to triumph in a world of lesser beings. Whether you are merely curious or are ready to roll up your sleeves and dig into hidden treasures, these are all presented here for your enjoyment and satisfaction. If you want a deeper understanding about what makes the male animal tick, this book is a must have! My deepest congratulations to Dr. Johnson for this groundbreaking work!

– Magister Nemo, BridgesToTruth.com

Nothing makes a woman revel in her feminine magic (and a Satanic Witch exercise her full power) more than the company of an equivalent Warlock counterpart. It's not a battle, it's a dance – reading this book will get men out of today's watered-down PC holding pattern and have them kicking up their heels and horns with fiery delight!

– Witch Karen Millman

What a treat this book has in store for you! This companion to *The Compleat Witch* is anything BUT just a companion piece. The Satanic Warlock is not a rewrite with "Witch" out and "Warlock" in. On these pages you will find an original, progressive, unabashed take on male sexuality from a Satanic perspective. Penned by one of the most devilishly sexy men I know, Bob Johnson will never disappoint... in any capacity!

– Magistra D. DeMagis

From the man known as "Hef with Horns," The Satanic Warlock is a refreshingly politically incorrect original treatise on the laws of attraction from the male perspective. This is an arsenal of tried, true, and tested knowledge, the result of years of experience playing the field. Learn the secrets to becoming a truly attractive, fascinating and sought-after male. Magister Bob Johnson is the only man I can think of appropriate to take on writing the companion to The Satanic Witch. He's stylish, original, and spot on!

– Magister Robert Lang

What you hold in your hand can only be described as one of the world's most authentic men's manuals. Sex, wealth and power can all be yours, but first you need to unlock them! Being born a Satanist is one thing, but being a successful Warlock takes unleashing the true animal within.

– Reverend John H. Shaw, Owner of iSatanist

Lightning Source UK Ltd.
Milton Keynes UK
UKHW01f1500020818
326679UK00001B/229/P